A New Approach
to
Language Arts
in the
Elementary School

Elvin Taylor

Parker Publishing Company, Inc.

West Nyack, New York

LIBRARY OF CONGRESS
CATALOG CARD NUMBER: 76-118698

PRINTED IN THE UNITED STATES OF AMERICA
ISBN-0-13-612408-9
B & P

How This Book
Can Help You

This book outlines a specific course of action to be followed by the teacher who is not satisfied with a language arts program which merely projects well-worn ideas and methods from conventional textbooks. It is directed towards the teacher who is capable of propelling the program successfully by the constant incorporation of new and ingenious ideas. A review of the many changes and specific examples of language arts units which have been used in successful classroom situations provides an interestingly new and optimistic look at the language arts program.

A logical sequential program is presented in the book to give elementary teachers a new and different approach to language arts. Whether the topic is open-minded, open-ended discussions, interviewing public officials, or taking part in worthwhile community social projects, the principal goal is to direct you to a greater depth in teaching. It is, in brief, a source book of practical, workable ideas for the busy teacher. This book will help you, the teacher, to become more involved in language arts. It will help you to analyze your present teaching methods and chart a new course of action. Interviews with educators, visits to classrooms, and personal experience in many phases of the educational field have been combined to focus interest on an improved language arts program.

Changes in language arts are discussed briefly in the early part of the book to provide an overall view of changes which have been effected and changes which can be expected in the near future. From this standpoint, the discussion is focused on specific areas of instruction: reading, language, creative writing, speech, critical writing, vocabulary, spelling, and evaluation. Under each of these topics, new techniques have been discussed, practical suggestions have been presented, and conclusions have been drawn.

It is impossible to give all the answers to any subject in a single book. An attempt to accomplish such a task would be naive. The aim of this author, however, is to give worthwhile examples, practical solutions to problems, and an outline of a program which can be expanded and adjusted to meet various classroom situations. Hopefully, such an approach will lead to further changes which will contribute to a meaningful, unified language arts curriculum.

E. T.

Contents

Chapter 3   Teaching the Student How to Study   41

Chapter 6   Teaching the Proper Use of Words   95

Chapter 9   Effective Writing
Assignments   144

Chapter 10   Building Reading Skills   155

1

Establishing the Basis
for an Effective
Language Arts Program

Language arts teachers understandably concentrate on teaching students to read, to write intelligibly, and to speak with a reasonable amount of clarity. However, language arts involves many more than these three basic areas.

The goals of a good language arts program for a student now entering kindergarten endeavor to teach him to read, to help him to understand what he reads, and to give him the tools he needs in order to form an opinion about the material he has read. It is not enough to teach him to read from a conventional reading text, supplemented with a few works of fiction. He needs to know how to read and understand written material from all areas of knowledge. In a good program, the child learns to read the newspaper, to select worthwhile articles from a wide selection of magazines; in fact, he learns to find his own reading material. He learns to use the *Reader's Guide*, the card catalogue, indexes, and other library aids.

The goals also include clear, creative, and concise writing. The language arts student needs to learn to express himself in order to establish an outlet for the expression of his feelings. And he learns that writing skills are practical. The letters he writes, announcements he will have to write for a club, or the minutes for a class meeting are examples of how every student will use his written skills. Through writing, too, he learns the mechanical aspects of a sentence and of a paragraph.

The third major area of language arts involves speaking and listening. The two are inseparable, for communication is an exchange of ideas. To communicate, we must listen and we must be able to organize our thoughts. An updated language arts program provides numerous opportunities for the student to speak, to dramatize, and to communicate.

The language arts student in a well-planned program learns, through reading, through study, and through direct observation, to judge character and to recognize examples of propaganda. He also learns to set goals for himself. The teacher helps him to do this by allowing him to make decisions, and to make judgments.

REQUIREMENTS FOR A GOOD LANGUAGE ARTS PROGRAM

In brief form, here are the criteria for a good language arts program:

1. A creative, open-minded teacher who plans, develops, and instigates new ideas and new teaching methods.
2. Access to an ample supply of audio-visual aids such as projectors, tape recorders, educational television, radios, overhead projectors, and individual learning machines.
3. A good learning atmosphere, a well-lighted, con-

veniently arranged room with movable equipment and plenty of space for visual materials.

4. Plenty of attractive, well-planned teacher-made and commercial audio-visual materials. (Many teachers develop their own tape recorded remedial and enrichment materials.)

5. Access to all types of library books and reference books, as well as magazines, papers, etc.

6. A good attitude of learning established by the teacher. (This involves gaining the confidence of the student and the cooperation of the parents and the administrators.)

7. An integrated language curriculum; that is, one which is very closely related to the other subject areas. For instance, some time should be taken in the science class, the socials studies class, etc. to teach students to write good sentences, write good paragraphs, to answer discussion questions, and do some research.

GOALS FOR THE LANGUAGE ARTS PROGRAM

Beginning with pre-school children, we must recognize that *ability levels differ*. For this reason, it is difficult for us to set limits of achievements for the various grade levels. It is, however, both possible and beneficial to set standards of achievement for various grades.

If there are not at least two, three, five students or more in an average sized kindergarten class who can read entire sentences as well as first, second, or third graders, by the time they have finished their first year of school, something is probably wrong with the kindergarten program. Similarly, if some of the sixth graders are not reading at least a limited amount of high school material, such as advanced magazines, etc., something is probably wrong with the language arts program at that level too. In other words, the good language arts program provides for a wide range of ability and achievement.

KINDERGARTEN

1. Learn the rules of common courtesy.
2. Learn to listen to directions.
3. Learn to follow directions.
4. Learn good listening habits.
   a. Listen as a story is read.
   b. Listen as someone else speaks. (Don't think about what you are going to say, but about what the other person is saying.)
5. Learn to tell a story or an incident in brief, organized form.
6. Learn to speak clearly.
7. Learn to read simple directives such as "Stop," "Walk Slowly," etc.
8. Learn to dramatize stories and story characters.
9. Learn to print your name correctly.
10. Learn to form all of the letters of the alphabet.
11. Learn some of the letter sounds. (Many teachers teach the sounds of all the letters of the alphabet to kindergarten students.)

GRADE 1

1. Learn all of the vowel and consonant sounds.
2. Learn to read books with a limited vocabulary.
3. Learn to read orally, using proper inflections, intonations, pauses, etc.
4. Learn to spell a limited number of words.
5. Learn to write complete sentences.
6. Learn to write at least three consecutive sentences related to one main idea.

7. Learn to follow more detailed directions.
8. Use experience charts for writing and organizational purposes.
9. Learn to make judgments. For instance, is he a good character?

GRADE 2

1. Learn to read books with a larger vocabulary.
2. Learn to relate orally an incident from a story or from personal experience in a clear and concise manner.
3. Learn to follow more explicit directions. For instance, assignment headings may be more detailed at this level.
4. Learn to listen more carefully and retain more of what you hear.
5. Learn to write longer sentences.
6. Second grades should continue to write two to four consecutive related sentences when the occasion for writing arises in the classroom.
7. Learn to write letters.
8. Learn to punctuate correctly.
9. Gain greater facility in oral language.

GRADE 3

1. Learn to write in cursive style.
2. Continue to read material which is increasingly difficult.
3. Begin to give more formal reports.
4. Keep book file cards on books they have read.
5. Their spoken and written vocabularies are increased.
6. Learn new aspects of spelling and pronuncia-

tion—the hyphen, accent marks, dictionary spellings, etc.
7. Write creative stories.

GRADE 4

1. Begin to use the library for actual, but limited, research.
2. Write well-organized paragraphs which include at least four good sentences.
3. Their creative stories will be longer and better organized.
4. Oral discussions will have more purpose and the students themselves will accept more responsibility for their organization.
5. Read full-length books.
6. Some will become interested in newspapers and magazines.
7. Write factual reports.
8. Learn to outline.
9. Become more independent in their work habits.
10. Be more expressive and more concise in their oral presentations.
11. Learn to use good study habits..

GRADE 5

1. Some students will be avid readers by this level.
2. They will learn larger and more specialized vocabularies for each subject area.
3. The newspaper becomes a part of the curriculum.
4. Encyclopedias, almanacs, dictionaries, and other reference materials will be used with much more frequency.
5. They will learn to read and study the material for each subject area, in a different way.

6. Independent research on special topics of interest will be done by the best students.

GRADE 6

1. Independent research is a very important part of the sixth grade curriculum.
2. Be able to spell a list of words, such as the following, correctly.
    a. saddle (double consonant)
    b. straight (silent letters)
    c. easily (changing the y to i)
    d. shaping (single consonant following the long A)
    e. joint (2 consonants together)
    f. weather-whether (distinguish between the two)
    g. caught-cot (homonyms)
    h. tomorrow (a single and a double consonant)
    i. committee (3 sets of double letters)
    j. niece (word often misspelled)
3. Writing
    a. Be able to write good sentences—varied, exciting, concise, expressive.
    b. Be able to write good paragraphs.
    c. Be able to make smooth transitions from paragraph to paragraph.
    d. Be able to write good and interesting friendly and business letters.
    e. Be able to express the answer to a thought question in a logical and concise manner.
    f. Be able to write a factual report without "copying" material.
    g. Be able to outline, using subtopics.
    h. Be able to observe something or someone and then describe what you have observed.

4. The library
   a. Be able to locate a book in any library.
   b. Be able to locate a magazine article by using *Reader's Guide*.
   c. Be familiar with and be able to use library reference books.
   d. Be able to do a limited amount of research.
5. Reading
   a. We read to learn and to understand. If a sixth grader can read and understand such books as *Red Pony, The Big Wave, A Light in the Forest* without difficulty, he is at least average in his reading skills.
   b. He should have an interest in reading. The sixth grade student should read at least one magazine article independently each week. He should read at least some part of a newspaper each day. He should read at least some type of a book, other than his assigned texts, each week.
   c. He should be able to relate the main ideas in a story after reading it.
   d. He should understand most of the vocabulary.

These goals are much the same as they have been in the past. Our methods, however, are different. Students pass into junior high school and even into college without achieving some of these goals. The language arts program must therefore attempt to give the student the tools with which he can meet most of these goals.

The language arts curriculum is now, more than ever, one of *doing*. Rather than spending a multitude of hours teaching grammar, grammar, grammar, we teach the various aspects of sentences and paragraphs through writing. When an error is made in a sentence, we find the cause of the error and attempt to correct it. We teach spelling in the same manner. As a student misspells a word, he is shown the correct spelling, and he is given part of the responsibility for learning the correct spelling, by keeping a "misspellings" chart.

The library work is made meaningful. Always the library assignments are to be full of interest so that the child will begin to use the library independently simply because he *wants* to learn. The list of reading possibilities is so broad that everyone can find books of interest. The emphasis, though, must be on learning to read by reading.

Independent thought is encouraged through the use of open-end questions, questions which the child uses as spring-boards from which he can form his own opinions.

THE OPEN-END QUESTION

Getting students to think for themselves is one of the primary tasks of the elementary school. For the most part, this end is not met by the objective type of oral and written questions, but through the use of what is often called the open-end question.

This type of question can be thought of as a funnel. It states a principle, concept, or generalization, and then allows the student to formulate his own conclusions. The question may or may not have an answer, or the student's answer may vary considerably from that of his classmates and still be acceptable. We are trying to inspire new ideas and creativity in the students. Leon Blum said, "The free man is he who does not fear to go to the end of his thought." Our goal, then, is to create free men.

Following are some examples of open-ended questions which can be used in the elementary school: (After reading a story)

1. Why did the main character accept defeat?
2. Was the main character closer to your view of a perfect or an imperfect man?
3. Which character in the story was your favorite? Why?

4. Why did you like or dislike the story?
5. What would *you* have done if you had been in the main character's place?

THE LANGUAGE ARTS PERIOD
IS A PARTICIPATION PERIOD

The entire school day is concerned with communication. The student reads from dozens of books, newspapers, and magazines. He reads directions, signs, and bulletin boards. He also listens to thousands of words and sounds each school day. Other portions of the day are spent in the output part of communications, speaking and writing. This part is being given more and more attention in today's language arts curriculums. Educators are trying to create a balance between intake (reading and listening) and output (speaking and writing). The student must be a participant in the program. He must increase his intake capacity if he is to balance what he has absorbed with active participation through creative writing, speech, and dramatics.

More and more, the language arts program is being filled with activities which have current as well as future value for the student. For instance, rather than writing letters to hypothetical people, write actual letters. During this process, the student will in most cases receive valuable information or material and at the same time learn letter writing skills. In dramatics, rather than searching the library for a suitable play, involve your students in play writing activities. But, all of the participation should not be writing. Have students choose stories and after practicing reading them, present them orally to the class. Making bulletin boards, taking surveys, studying advertising, and writing original poetry, are only a few ways language arts can be made a participation period.

OUT OF NOTHING, NOTHING COMES (ROMAN PROVERB)

Don't put the student in the dilemma of going somewhere, just for the sake of going. He must have goals. He must have direction. Too often, a student must feel like an amoeba. He is asked to go forward as far as he can, then when he encounters an obstruction, he must stop, move backwards, and try again in another area. This type of program often frustrates the student. Each teacher, however, must modify any educational plan to meet the requirements of his own classroom environment.

LANGUAGE ARTS AS A BASIS FOR THE CURRICULUM

The student's language arts training to a large extent will determine how well he will do in other subject areas. The study of history, science, and even math, demand proficiency in reading comprehension. Adeptness in the social sciences requires a sizable amount of knowledge of dictionary skills, library skills, and a suitable vocabulary. Problem solving skills are important in all of the academic areas. A thorough knowledge of all of these skills is most likely to result from a concentrated effort to teach language arts as a whole, plus an attempt to interrelate language arts with the entire curriculum. There is a growing tendency to judge an entire educational program by the effectiveness of the language arts program. Does it have a "humanizing" effect on the child? Does it help him to develop socially? Does it provide the skills vital to the understanding of the other subject areas?

CHECK LIST FOR THE LANGUAGE ARTS PROGRAM

1. The language arts program teaches the basic reading, writing, and speaking skills.

2. It teaches independence in research.
3. It teaches the student to express his ideas and feelings concisely.
4. It teaches critical judgment.
5. It takes into consideration the total needs of the child.
6. It is a well-planned program for developing necessary skills and interests.
7. It teaches him to think clearly and logically, forming his *own* opinions.
8. The student learns through participation.
9. Both the students and the teacher establish goals.
10. Language arts serves as a basis for the curriculum.

2

Developing Communication
Skill in Language Arts

The purpose of the curriculum is to develop many skills which will be of use to the elementary student. These skills include oral, written, and oral-written skills in language arts. Whether we do it consciously or not, we rely on these skills each time we attempt to communicate our thoughts and ideas. They are the crutches we use thousands of times each day to make life more meaningful. Oral skills are learned first, forming the foundation for written skills.

This chapter includes discussions of several basic language arts skills which have not been considered at length elsewhere in the book. It assumes the premise that to be successful in school, to participate in community affairs, to communicate with family and friends, and to enjoy and benefit from these activities, a child needs skill in all of the following language areas: speaking correctly and effectively before groups, conversing adequately with others, using the correct techniques of handwriting, being able to write letters properly, and listening with a purpose.

CLEAR, CONCISE SPEECH

Since most people express themselves much more often by speaking than by writing, training for correct speech is extremely important in the elementary curriculum. Many of the child's speech patterns have already been formed long before he comes to school, but it is the task of the school to help the child correct faulty speech habits, develop confidence in his own speech, and to learn to express himself as correctly as possible. Clinical speech defects are in the realm of specialists and do not usually concern the classroom teacher.

Goals of the Speech Program

1. To learn to express ideas correctly and concisely.
2. To express opinions and ideas in a manner which encourages others to listen.
3. To learn to manipulate the voice to best advantage in many speaking situations.
4. To be confident before, yet sensitive to, an audience.

Speech Problems in the Classroom

Students in the lower grades who speak improperly are not usually aware of their faulty speech habits. Awareness of the problem, then, comes first. Only awareness which is accomplished not by embarrassment, but by understanding the problem, followed by competent guidance in overcoming the problem, is helpful.

Some of the problems with which classroom teachers have to deal are weak vocalization, faulty pronunciation of words by omitting and substituting letter sounds, accenting the wrong syllable of a word, speaking too rapidly or too slowly, speaking in a monotone, etc. These are problems which result in poor communication or a lack of communication altogether. Children do not automatically become good speakers. They must be trained to speak correctly.

The teacher's speech is the first step in student awareness of a speech problem. The teacher must be aware constantly of correct speech as students both consciously and unconsciously model their speech after their teacher. In the case of many students with faulty speech habits, they will notice very early that the teacher pronounces some of his words in a different way than he does. From this point, these same students will begin to experiment with their own speech and they will attempt to conform to standards of acceptable speech. But for most students, much more is necessary in teaching correct oral communication than being a model of correct speech.

USING THE TAPE RECORDER   For the student, no device and no technique makes him so aware of the strong points and the weaknesses of his own oral communication as does the tape recorder. One of its main advantages is that it can be used very successfully at every level of the curriculum. Many kindergarten teachers use it and find it very helpful in early speech improvement.

Many teachers apply the speak-listen experimental technique in their classrooms to reveal to students the characteristics of their speech. If possible, it is usually best, to avoid embarrassment, to record the student's voice, either while he is not aware of the recorder, or while he is alone or in a small group. Earphones will make it possible for him to listen to his own voice individually. The initial reaction a student usually has to a first-time recording of his voice is that it doesn't sound like his own voice. Older students will probably already have learned the reason for this—that only part of the sound vibrations produced in the throat are carried through the air, and that the other sound vibrations which we ourselves hear travel in the head from the vocal cords to the inner ear, thus creating a different sound from that which others hear. Soon, though, the student will overcome any fear he might have had of his own voice and through teacher-student cooperation, the individual problems can be isolated and an attempt can be made to correct them. The following paragraphs discuss some of the common speech difficulties and the teacher's role in correcting these difficulties.

LETTER OMISSIONS AND SUBSTITUTIONS   During a period of observation of student speech, a teacher may note letter omissions similar to the following which elementary students frequently make:

"were" for where
"wat" for what
"goin" for going
"drif" for drift
"col" for cold
"everday" for everyday

How will the teacher proceed in attempting to correct these and similar errors? One procedure is to listen and record on the blackboard, as a class, mistakes of this nature made during a short period when students are doing most of the speaking. (Unless care is taken though, students may become so involved in listening for mistakes that they will forget to listen for content.) For the lower grades it is helpful to have the class practice pronouncing the words correctly as a group. Sometimes, having the students overemphasize the deleted letter when repeating the word which was incorrectly pronounced helps prevent the student from repeating his mistake. The same procedure can be followed when letters are added or substituted in words, as in this brief list:

"often" for of n
"tumbeling" for tumbling
"pernounce" for pronounce

ACCENTING THE WRONG SYLLABLE   Accenting the wrong syllable is a problem which virtually all people encounter with some words at one time or another. Even some newscasters have trouble with some words such as formidable. The lower elementary student will be confused with such terms as primary and secondary accents and little will be gained by attempts to teach technicalities such as these at this level. However, the same purpose can be accomplished by a more basic procedure. Write the accented syllable in large letters. For instance:

disPOSE

colLAPSE

INfamous

EXtract or exTRACT

reMEMber

Use this procedure only with words which the students mispronounce. It is pointless to set out to write an entire list of words which students are neither interested in nor can relate to themselves. Such an activity is boring and holds little meaning for them.

SPEED, VOCALIZATION, AND VOICE VARIETY   These three speech difficulties can be corrected most easily if the student can hear his own voice by means of a recorder. But, even with a recorder, a great deal of practice is necessary. If possible, the student should practice alone a great deal, often repeating a short paragraph several times until no mistakes are made. He will need to learn to change his speed and pitch frequently to avoid monotony. Overemphasizing pitch change and voice variety when practicing helps many students improve their speech.

SENSITIVITY TO THE AUDIENCE   One of the main language needs of children is to overcome embarrassment when speaking before a group. Before a child can completely overcome this embarrassment, though, he must have confidence in his own voice and in what he has to say. He must believe that what he has to say will be of value to the audience; he must be sensitive enough to his audience to prevent offense; he must experiment and practice with his voice until he is fully aware of his own vocal capabilities.

The young child usually experiences much less embarrassment before an audience than does an adolescent who has not had a good background in oral communication; he has not practiced bad language habits for so long. If the child, with the teacher's help, can develop a keen interest in what he has to say before a group, his interest will often supersede his embarrassment and he will be able to communicate successfully to his audience. As children are learning to speak correctly, the teacher can inject at the proper time many helpful hints for the young speaker. After the class has had some practice in speaking, a set of rules for the speaker should be developed. The following standards are appropriate for students in the elementary grades. In fact, the same basic ideas also apply to older students.

STANDARDS FOR THE SPEAKER For students in grades kindergarten through second, the teacher's concern is more with getting the child to express himself. Too many do's and don'ts at this level will hamper expression of ideas. Inducing the child to express himself and to communicate freely is still of prime concern in the third to sixth grade group, but gradually, certain standards must be interjected, as the higher the level of the audience, the more critical they become, and failure to follow accepted standards for speaking may result in a lack of communication.

1. Appearance is important. Practice good posture, but avoid stiffness. Try to look relaxed. One foot should be slightly ahead of the other so that you can maintain good balance.
2. Don't look at the floor or at the ceiling, but directly at your audience.
3. Speak loudly enough so that everyone in the audience can hear you. Don't speak too loudly though.
4. Avoid movements or mannerisms which will distract or annoy the audience—for instance, shifting from foot to foot, twisting the hands, or swinging the arms.
5. Be sure that what you have to say is important enough that the audience will want to listen to you.

6. Breathe properly. Don't breathe in the middle of
   a sentence.

Speaking Practice

Much of the practice in speaking should be part of the curriculum, taking the form of spontaneous class responses, assigned and volunteer individual reports and speeches, and interviews, panel discussions, and other speech experiences either in language arts or in some other related subject area.

For the primary grades, oral language practice consists primarily of spontaneous class responses such as in conversation periods and show and tell activities. Students in the intermediate grades, however, are expected to respond individually to the whole group in a more formal speaking situation and at greater length than the primary students. For instance, a third or fourth grade assignment might be a one minute report on "My favorite T.V. program, season, holiday, food, etc." Or it might be "A new experience I had," "An exciting game," "An interesting place to visit." Most of the topics at this level should be related quite closely to the speaker.

At the fifth–sixth grade level, many of the individual reports and speeches will be somewhat longer—two to four minutes. The topics in these grades will also change. They will be more comprehensive, and often they will include more judgments and opinions than do reports in earlier grades. Topics might be: "Whom do I admire most?", "America's number one hero!", "Early pioneers (science, exploration, etc.)."

Here is a brief outline of the speech program in elementary school:

Kindergarten through second grade—Spontaneous speech: conversation, the basics of telephoning, reports of trips, new discoveries—all in an informal setting. The teacher at this level will try to establish an air of freedom in this phase of the language curriculum. The student must want to speak because what he has to say seems important to him.

Grades three and four—Still stress free play of ideas, conduct discussions, group choral projects, but some formal speeches should be made at this level; that is, speaking before a group. The speeches should be short, usually about one minute.

Grades five and six—The speeches at this level are longer and more comprehensive; that is, they involve more difficult topics and they require keener judgment.

If students in these grades are reluctant to speak individually to an audience, it is sometimes helpful to allow joint speaking projects—two students jointly giving a speech, one covering one part of the topic, the other the rest of the topic. This is one way to help students gain more confidence in their speech.

Evaluating the Speech

Evaluation is a vital part of the speech program. Students need and want to know the effect of their speech on the audience. After most class speeches or reports, the teacher will give the student either a brief oral or written evaluation of his speech. It is also important that the other students occasionally have an opportunity to evaluate the speaker. Answering one or more of such questions as the following indicates to the speaker the effectiveness of his speech:

1. I liked the speech because. . . .
2. I was not interested in the report because. . . .
3. The part of the report I liked most was. . . .
4. I liked the (beginning, ending) of the report better.
5. I would rate the report (poor, good, excellent).

CONVERSATION

Every segment of the language arts curriculum should have immediate value for the student. Since conversation does have immediate value for the student at school as well as away from school, it should definitely have a place in the curriculum. Most elementary students have developed a degree of proficiency in conversation by frequent use, but there are few elementary aged children who do not need to improve their conversation abilities.

The lower elementary teacher provides for conversation as a part of the curriculum. Unfortunately, this provision is not always made in the intermediate grades. Thus many students develop poor habits of conversation. When trying to develop and improve conversation skills, it is helpful to listen to interesting taped conversation excerpts. These provide a basis for discussion and models for the students. For many students, a well-chosen listening activity such as this will encourage better listening and a keener interest in carrying on conversations. A set of conversation standards developed by the class should include the following:

1. Remember the purpose of conversation—a worthwhile exchange of ideas.
2. No one should monopolize the conversation—listen as well as contribute to the conversation.
3. Stick to the point, avoiding abrupt changes of the subject.
4. Avoid statements such as "You are wrong!"
5. Make no unfounded statements.
6. Discuss, don't argue.
7. Make only worthwhile contributions to the conversation.

Conversation Activities

1. Tape one-sided conversations, such as a telephone conversation. The students fill in the missing part.
2. Divide the class into groups of three to five students. Each group is given a topic or they are allowed to choose their own topic. The group

carries on a conversation for about three minutes. Each group presents a brief synopsis of its conversation.

HANDWRITING

Extended teaching of handwriting after the basic techniques have been learned seems to this author to be successful only if the training is individualized enough to single out and help improve the principal mistakes each student makes. One student may have difficulty in forming the letters while another may need to concentrate on improving "r." The handwriting of one student may be too large, and that of another too small. Because of the difficulty left-handers often have in writing, they also should receive special help.

There are conflicting ideas regarding the length of time taken from the day's schedule to teach handwriting. Some teachers feel that a daily handwriting class is indispensable, while the extreme view advocates no formal handwriting classes. Others favor fewer class periods and more stress on writing in the other classes. Depending on the abilities of his own class, the individual teacher must make a judgment on the type of program which will best meet the needs of his students.

WRITING LETTERS

Writing good letters is an art which the student must learn. All of the practice necessary for reinforcing letter writing techniques can and must come through actual letters. Business letters requesting material for some class project, thank-you letters, letters of congratulation, and friendly letters all have a part in language arts. Letters written to the editor of various student newspapers and magazines can help teach good writing techniques. This last letter writing activity can also teach the uniqueness of our governmental system which permits free expression.

Letter Writing Activities

Here are some situations which call for letter writing in the classroom:

I. For a field trip
   A. A letter of request to visit the bakery, etc.
   B. A follow-up letter acknowledging the reply
   C. A thank-you letter sent after the visit

II. During a study of a different state or city
   A. A letter suggesting an exchange of information about the different region
   B. A second letter acknowledging the reply and the first exchange of information
   C. Students continue the exchange of letters past this point individually if they wish

III. A speaker to the classroom
   A. A request that he visit the room
   B. A letter of appreciation for his visit

IV. Placing an order
   A. The students order a book or magazine for the class library using class funds
   B. If shipping or other problems arise, a follow-up letter should be sent.

LISTENING SKILLS

Listening is such a very important language skill that it cannot simply be taken for granted. Analyze your class and decide what listening skills they need to learn.

1. Does the class concentrate on what is being said so that they understand the ideas the first time they hear them?
2. Are your directions and explanations so long and

involved that they have no interest for the students?

3. Do you give students ample opportunity to be "the speaker"?
4. Do they understand that listening is as important as speaking?
5. Do they listen critically, questioning the truth and the worth of what has been said?
6. Are they really listening or are they "with you" physically only?

To Develop Listening Skills

1. Prepare or find interesting paragraphs or short articles and insert some place in the text, ideas, facts, or grammatical constructions which are incorrect. Students listen carefully to detect the mistake.
2. After listening to weather reports, newscasts, or other reports, check the accuracy of what they have heard.
3. Ask questions only once to encourage them to become sharp listeners.
4. Use the tape recorder in teaching listening. Record a series of sounds, such as a door closing, water boiling, a clock ticking, or paper tearing. Ask students to identify these sounds.
5. Listen and draw. Read a description to the students and ask them to draw it.
6. The teacher reads a short paragraph—a news story, directions, a description, etc. The reading stops abruptly in the middle of a sentence or at a critical point in the paragraph and the students try to determine, using what they have heard, what will come next in the paragraph. A recorded speech may be used and the recorder stopped at

a particular place and the same procedure followed.

PROOFREADING

Proofreading is a very important language arts skill which students can acquire best by analyzing their own written work. Everything written in the classroom should be proofread at least once. Here is a set of standards for proofreading:

1. Have you followed the rules for correct punctuation, capitalization and spelling?
2. Are your letters formed correctly and is your writing legible?
3. Did you indent where necessary?
4. What is the general appearance of your paper?
5. Have you put the proper heading at the top of your paper?
6. Have you completed the assignment?

MORE PRACTICE

A. For a day, or a week, designate a newsboy or newsgirl. The duties of the news person will be to give announcements to the class which are pertinent. For older students, integrate language arts with social studies by having the newsperson give news announcements which are of local, national, or international importance.

B. In connection with the school paper, class report, etc., interview one of the school personnel, a classmate, a student from another class, a parent, or a cooperative community worker. Be sure you follow the rules for correct interviews.

Know what you are going to ask before the interview. Record responses accurately. Don't ask embarrassing questions. Make the interview as brief and as comprehensive as possible.

C. Conduct a panel discussion in science or some other subject area.

D. Introduce visitors and speakers to the room.

E. Give interesting class reports whenever they are pertinent.

CHECK LIST FOR LANGUAGE ARTS SKILLS

1. The nature and number of speech problems are determined.
2. The tape recorder, individual attention, and well-directed practice are means of correcting speech deficiencies.
3. A list of standards for the speaker is established.
4. The students evaluate the speaker.
5. They learn the "give and take" of conversation.
6. They are involved in many conversation activities.
7. They are involved in letter writing activities. They write letters for *real* situations and mail them.
8. Teaching handwriting is a constant process. Each teacher must be alert to errors in letter formation, even flow of letters, etc. The students attempt to correct these errors on an individual basis.
9. Students learn to listen as a part of their language arts training.
10. Proofreading is an important skill to be learned in elementary school.
11. Practice is necessary to reinforce these skills.

3

Teaching the Student
How to Study

Is it possible to attend grade school, junior high school, and senior high school without actually learning how to study? Yes, it is, and many college freshmen "drop-outs" attest to this fact. Various people are blamed for this weakness in the curriculum, but perhaps elementary teachers should be given more of the blame than they now accept. Many students never learn how to study.

Study skills should be learned very early. These study skills not only include use of reference books, library skills, and such skills as indexing, but they also include the knowledge of how to study. This means teacher-student cooperation in setting goals and carrying them out.

For a child to learn to study correctly he must be motivated enough to want to learn. He must see a purpose—a plan developed and carried out by an industrious and creative teacher. The plan, if it is to be successful, will contain useful and exciting assignments with which the child can relate.

In this chapter many of the study skills are discussed. All

of them are important and the goals, assignments, and approaches considered can lead to more valuable learning for the student.

THE INDEX

The main purpose for teaching index skills to an elementary student is to encourage fast and efficient location of topics in which the student has an interest and for which he has a need. Learning to use an index should begin very early in elementary school. This skill should be taught at a time coinciding with the first use of indexes in textbooks and other curriculum materials being used. By this time the child should have acquired some skill in alphabetizing. Index skills should be taught in the lower grades and reinforced through use for the rest of the elementary years.

Teaching the Child to Use an Index

Direct experience—examining indexes and making their own—is the best and only effective way a child can learn to use an index. The classroom and the library contain many good examples of indexes for study. The telephone directory, the newspaper, the library card catalogue, and many books on the primary child's level contain indexes which are material for study. Finding their own names or names of friends in the telephone directory is often the first experience a child has with an index.

Learning to use an index requires a number of skills. They are given here in the form of a check list.

1. *Learning to alphabetize.*
2. *Learning the location of an index.* In the majority of texts and reference books, the index is located at the end of the book. One major exception is the *World Almanac* which, because of the extensive use of the index in a reference of this type, is

located at the front of the book. In newspapers, it may be on the first or second page.

3. *Understanding the purpose of an index.* The main purpose of an index is to locate rapidly topics, events, and names of people and places.

4. *Distinguishing between an index and a glossary.* A glossary is an alphabetized list of defined terms closely associated with the material in the book. It is usually found just before the index, but in some cases it takes the place of the index.

5. *The purpose and location of an appendix.* An appendix is located just before the index and it may include explanatory tables, explanations of parts of the texts, or other pertinent information which has no defined place in the text.

6. *The physical features of an index.*
   a. It is alphabetized.
   b. It is organized with main headings and subheadings, each accompanied by a page number.
   c. Many indexes are quite comprehensive while others are brief and inadequate.

Practice with an Index

I.   An early class indexing project is to have the class alphabetize the names of students in the room in an attractive manner and then place the list in a prominent place in the room. The names should be written in large letters on a large piece of oak tag or other suitable material.

II.   The same procedure may be used in indexing hobbies in the room. After a class discussion of hobbies, let the class make their own index. In this type of outline index, the names of the hobbies are the main index headings with the students' names used as the subheadings. Both the hobbies and the names under each hobby should be alphabetized. If a student has more than one hobby, enter his name in the index more than once. Point out that while a particular main topic is entered only once in the index, the same subheading may appear many times under several different main topics. Let students find examples of this.

III.   *Making a file.* Examine several files such as the card files in the library, professional files, etc. The class should decide on a topic they would like to index in a card file. Possible topics are:

a. Places we have visited

b. A picture file of important people

c. Stories and/or books we have read

IV.   *Special topic files such as "New Scientific Discoveries," "History in the Making."* This file is one which can include either newspaper and magazine clippings or short written reports.

V.   Another type of class file is one which is a part of the entire year's work in language arts. It is organized to meet the needs of one particular classroom and it may include such main topics as writing, poetry, literature. It may include copies of reports, class goals, analyses of projects, etc. This type of file is a record of the year's work and it can be used effectively for periodic reviews.

REFERENCES AND HOW TO USE THEM

The Dictionary

The most basic of reference books is the dictionary. The first American dictionary, written by Noah Webster at the beginning of the nineteenth century, contained only a fraction of the words which are included in today's current dictionaries. Now there are over one million words, counting all of the words and their forms, in existence in the English language. An unabridged dictionary contains far fewer than one million words and the child's versions contain only a few.

A good dictionary not only lists the words with their basic meanings, but it gives many nuances or shades of meanings of many words. It also gives such information as the origin of the word, the part of speech, different forms of the word, pictorial explanations for some words, and in the case of some children's dictionaries, a sentence showing correct use of the word is given.

Here is a check list for dictionary skills:

1. Learning the alphabet and gaining skill in alphabetizing
2. Learning to use the dictionary guide words
3. Understanding dictionary symbols (diacritical marks)
4. Understanding word roots
5. Learning to interpret dictionary respellings
6. Learning to select and use the correct definitions
7. Locating specific data other than word meanings (plurals, parts of speech, deviant spellings, etc.)
8. Interpreting dictionary abbreviations
9. Learning to use cross references
10. Learning word derivations
11. Understanding supplementary materials included in the dictionary

WORD MEANINGS   The first dictionary skill which we will discuss is that of finding word meanings. This is the skill for which a child can first recognize a need, and therefore, it should be introduced at the first grade level. Pictorial dictionaries, glossaries, and other types of simple dictionaries give students experience in finding and using word meanings. It is desirable in all grades to have one dictionary for each student. As a difficult word is encountered, students can use their personal dictionary to locate the word, and certainly as the skill is being learned, the word will be located by all of the students with the help of the teacher. Soon, though, some students will be able to locate the words themselves, and they will be concerned with learning other dictionary skills.

In beginning dictionaries, the words are concrete; that is, they name people, things, and places which can be touched, or seen, or shown in a picture. Let's suppose a lower elementary class has just encountered a word such as HOTEL. Perhaps no one can give an entirely accurate definition of the word, so the teacher decides to make use of the dictionary. If possible, an opaque projector or an overhead projector should be used by the teacher, while the students follow in their dictionaries. The following procedure can be used effectively with most lower elementary classes:

1. Give the page number where the word can be found.
2. Let students examine the word and definition. They will immediately see the value of a dictionary even though they were not able to find the word themselves.
3. Help them discover that all of the words are in alphabetical order.
4. Teach the use of the guide words. Some students will soon be finding words in their dictionaries very rapidly. Others will need a great deal of practice.

By third grade, students will be encountering a number of more difficult words such as COMMUNITY, MUSEUM, and BUSINESS. These words are more difficult because understanding their meanings means understanding several concepts. For instance, a museum contains old things and items of value. Tourists visit a museum. A museum is usually a public place. The upper primary grades and intermediate grade students will learn that words have more than one meaning. They will learn that some animals also live in communities.

A SOURCE OF INFORMATION   There are numerous dictionary activities which give the student practice with the

dictionary. The following are questions which the student can answer with a good dictionary:
1. Where is Pompeii?
2. How long was Thomas Jefferson president of the United States?
3. What is the correct way to pronounce *draught?*
4. How did the opossum get its name?
5. From which language did the word *levee* come?

MORE PRACTICE   Use a good synonym dictionary—*Soule's Dictionary of English Synonyms* is an excellent reference book—to find a colorful word to fill the following blanks:
1. The hungry dogs_____their food.
2. The chairman_____the desk.
3. The pitcher_____the ball across the park.
4. Angry rioters_____through the darkened streets.
5. The students_____excitedly as they left the classroom.
6. The car swerved_____as it turned the corner.
7. We watched as the_____jet rose gracefully into the sky.

To summarize, the dictionary is used principally to:
1. Find the main definition and variant meanings of words.
2. Find and check the correct spelling of a word.
3. Find the root of a word and other forms of the word.
4. Find pronunciations.

The Encyclopedia

Some of the skills needed in using an encyclopedia are:
1. Finding words alphabetically
2. Using an index (Most encyclopedias do not have

a single index, but topics are arranged in alphabetical order throughout.)
3. Using cross references
4. Using guide words
5. Updating an encyclopedia (Insert dates of deaths, new discoveries, etc.)
6. Using the encyclopedia to validate material in textbooks, newspapers, etc. (Children should be critical readers and not accept everything that is printed without checking another source.)

Educators realize that one of the major educational tasks is that of teaching students to locate information. One way of accomplishing this is to assign topics pertinent to the students and let them proceed to write their own condensed explanation of the topic. To add interest to this assignment, students may exchange outlines before writing the short reports. Occasionally students should listen as an article is read from an encyclopedia, taking only necessary notes, and then drawing from what they have heard and the notes they have taken, write their outline and report. To make this assignment meaningful, though, choose topics of interest to the students such as topics relating to American Indians, cave men, exotic animals, etc.

The Almanac

The almanac is one of the most important single-volume reference books in existence. Such information as news chronologies, statistics from recent census reports, biographical data on famous people, and geographical facts can be found in it. Most almanacs are published annually and can be purchased in paperback form.

Use of the almanac can and should begin in the fifth and sixth grades and for some students it may begin even before this level. Not only does the almanac offer valuable information on almost every subject, but it provides practice with the index. Several almanacs should be available in the classroom for student use.

One important use students can make of the almanac is that of comparison. Often the statistics and much of the other information in an encyclopedia is outdated soon after publication but since the almanacs are published annually, they are often more reliable. Since reference books occasionally disagree on important information, the almanac can be used as another source for comparison.

The following are questions which students may answer with the almanac when such information is pertinent to an area of study:

1. What was the population of Pennsylvania in 1790? (Look under U.S. Statistics)
2. What is Wisconsin's nickname? (See States)
3. What is the distance between Chicago and Los Angeles? (Air Distance)
4. What is the longitude and latitude of London, England? (Longitude and Latitude)
5. When was NATO established? (Treaties)
6. Where was Richard Byrd born? (Famous People)
7. Where were the Olympic games held in 1960? (Olympic Games)
8. In mythology, who was Atlas? (Mythology)
9. The Constitution has_____ amendments. (U.S. Constitution)

Other References

There are many other types of reference material aside from the three references already discussed—the dictionary, the encyclopedia, the almanac. Sometimes though, due to a weakness in the curriculum, they are not used to any extent in the elementary classroom.

THE LIBRARY The bare minimum of time spent by a class in the school or public library should be one class period for the intermediate grades. Much of this time should be spent getting acquainted with the materials there. When a student becomes bored with the library, it may be because he is not aware of all of the types of information and sources available there. Take for example these discoveries made by a fifth grade class during a single visit to the library.

1. Tom found his older brother's name listed in the Denver, Colorado, telephone directory.
2. Mary and Carol found and read the accounts of the 1960 national election in the newspaper room.
3. Mike and Roger found and read old newspaper and magazine articles telling of the Pearl Harbor attack.
4. Linda and John listened to recordings in the listening section of the library.
5. Mark, an amateur stamp collector, located several new books on his hobby.
6. Larry spent his time in the children's magazine section.
7. Alan, Donna, and Randy checked out books they hadn't read before.

Spending time in the library locating materials themselves gives students a sense of independence and accomplishment. As soon as they have learned to use an index they can use the card file of children's books to find out which books are available. It is one of the teacher's responsibilities to help children to discover the library; that is, to become familiar with all of its aspects and to use it as much as possible.

OTHER STUDY SKILLS

The Notebook

What should be kept in the student's notebook? Only information, tables, graphs, etc. which will have future value for the student. In social studies, for instance, many teachers follow the practice of making a brief outline of the day's discussion on the overhead projector, as the students supply the main headings. This type of information, even for the elementary students, is important as a review.

Too often an elementary class develops a set of goals or guidelines, writes reports, and constructs information tables without giving these important records of experiences a permanent place in student notebooks, class learning files, etc. Keeping records of this kind need not be as some teachers insist—boring or of no value. The above activities *do* become very tiresome to the student when he has to reconstruct guidelines again and again, and search for the same information repeatedly. Frequently the elementary student, particularly in the intermediate grades, is asked to review some subject material which has been discussed earlier. For instance, in social studies, he may need to review the study of the southeastern states. If he has not kept notes of any kind on the study, he finds himself in a very frustrating situation. With a well-organized notebook, the student has much of this information at his fingertips.

One of the most valuable aspects of a notebook is that a child can set aside a separate section of the notebook for his own special project. Each time he learns more about the topic he records it in his notebook. Unfortunately, this type of project is carried out by only a few of the better students as it requires a great deal more self-motivation than many students have.

Most of the material placed in the notebook should be in outline form or in diary style, or it may be in the form of brief notes. In the diary style notebook, used less frequently than the other types mentioned, the student writes a brief paragraph or two about skills learned in a unit just completed. He may keep a record of rules, important ideas he wants to remember, etc.

Taking Notes

Taking notes has a definite place in the elementary school. Often note-taking in the elementary school is given practically no attention and in many cases it is considered only haphazardly. One of the purposes of taking notes is, of course, to help us remember facts, ideas, etc. which we have heard and read. Surely, there must be information and procedures which elementary students should be expected to write down for future reference.

In the first, second, and third grades, note-taking is usually a group project in the form of experience charts or comparable records. In the case of directions, at all grade levels, an outline of specific procedures is constructed.

Rules for taking notes:
1. Write down only important ideas.
2. Don't concentrate so hard on writing down notes that you forget to listen to what is really being said.
3. Use underlining to indicate ideas which were stressed.
4. Don't record every word except for rules, laws, and quotations.
5. For easy reference, take notes on file cards.

These rules should have been learned and put into practice by the end of the sixth grade.

Begin to teach students the technique of note-taking by explaining the purpose of each activity:
1. Facts and ideas and quotations are important, and jotting them down gives the reader or listener a record which makes remembering them easier.

2. When listening to a speaker, you may wish to question a particular statement. Writing the question enables you to remember the statement and your question.
3. Notes can give you a basis for an outline from which a paragraph and the story or theme can be built.
4. Taking notes properly from material you read eliminates the unacceptable practice of copying word for word what someone else has already written.

Note-taking practice:

1. Invite a speaker to your room and note important ideas. Make a note of questions you wish to ask him after he is finished with his report.
2. Panel discussions, club meeting notes, taped newscasts, T.V. lessons, etc. are all opportunities for taking notes.

The Experience Chart

An experience chart is a forerunner to the outline. It is a brief, chronological listing of some class activity. It is usually written by the teacher on large sheets of paper with one idea expressed per line. A field trip calls for an experience chart. In the third grade, after a book has been read jointly, a class list of "things to remember" is often written.

The Outline

As soon as students have acquired the basic skills of reading, writing, etc., the teacher should give some direction in organizing material learned. Usually, though, outlining by individual students does not begin until the fourth grade, but it should certainly begin no later. Outlining is one of the best methods of teaching the child to organize what has been learned and what he anticipates learning. Some of the purposes of outlining are:

1. It provides a method for the child to organize material.
2. It helps the child become a more logical thinker.
3. It gives him a basis for good study later.
4. An outline is a handy reference.

First outlines, after experience charts, should be quite simple. Here are some examples of assignments:

1. Give three important ideas from the book "_____."
2. List four ways language develops.
3. Give five rules for writing good letters.

The outline in the elementary grades should be as useful as possible. An intermediate outline for a report might look like this:

GIRAFFE

tallest animal (may be 18 ft. tall)
Africa—native habitat
has long tongue for eating twigs and leaves
has two short horns
can see in all directions without moving his head
once known as camelopard because of its resemblance to the camel and leopard
has only seven vertebrae or bones in his neck
fast runner

In teaching outlining, remember:

1. Too much stress on outlining may cause the assignments to be ineffective.
2. First outlines built by the teacher on an overhead projector while the students plan and watch them develop are effective in teaching this skill.
3. Informal outlines can be very effective.
4. Even sixth graders should not be expected to develop highly detailed outlines.

5. Outlining can be used to a degree in most areas of the curriculum.

HOW TO STUDY

I. The Teacher's Responsibility

The teacher has an important responsibility in teaching students to study correctly. Thousands of students are inhibited in classrooms by irrelevant assignments—assignments that result in poor work, or at best, something which is mediocre. These assignments are not conducive to the learning and practice of good study skills. On the other hand, students thrive on meaningful assignments—learning to do—doing to learn exercises. What is the difference between worthwhile and less than worthwhile assignments? A requisite question for every entry in the plan book: "Does it relate to the student?" For students to learn the basic study skills and use them as a foundation for a well-developed program of study, their efforts must be channeled in meaningful directions.

Here is a list of assignments which can improve learning:

1. *Tactful Speech.* What would you say if someone said to you:
   a. Yours was the worst speech I ever heard.
   b. I don't like your coat.
   c. You are stupid if you believe him.
2. Write a letter to the student newspaper or news magazine and express your opinion about one of the recent articles.
3. *Conduct your own poll.* After examining several examples of recent polls, choose a topic which interests you and conduct your own poll. Decide on the scope of your poll—age limits, number polled, questions to be asked. If it is to be a poll of other students, you might ask questions about

favorite books, playground rules, or improving
the elementary band.

4. A "You should know that" class period in which
   students contribute useful facts, current news of
   interest to the class, and opinions.

5. Students write and tape their own news or other
   type of broadcast for other students to listen to.

II. Student Goals

To study effectively, one's goals must be carefully directed. Every student would do well to periodically deline-
ate his goals to himself—either in written or oral form. One
teacher of my acquaintance had a successful method of accomplishing this in her classroom. She asked students to
analyze themselves and their goals and record their discoveries. At the outset, however, she explained that no one
would read the reports but themselves. Recognizing that
much of what students write is designed to please the in-
structor, she felt this was the best approach. She found to
her surprise that many of the students wrote prolifically on
the topic. Results of this assignment were most rewarding.
Many of the students applied themselves much more ar-
dently in their work after they had given form to their goals.
But, whatever the method, students should be given ample
time and persuasion to channel their goals effectively. One
student list of goals included the following:

1. To learn to be a good speaker.
2. To learn to write good letters.
3. To read many interesting books and stories.
4. To learn about the library.
5. To become a good speller.

Rules for Study

I. Try to develop and maintain a healthy attitude towards study. This involves tolerance. You cannot afford to

dislike a subject simply because of physical factors such as an unpleasant room. Analyze your unfavorable attitudes as they develop and combat them in the most logical ways. Perhaps a discussion with the teacher would be helpful. Perhaps the root of your distaste for the course lies in your incompetency in the field. If so, you can help solve your problem with concentrated study in that particular area.

II. Keep a running list of work to be accomplished: homework, reports, discussions, etc. As each assignment is completed, check it off the list.

III. Organize your entire day around a schedule. Be sure you have a balance of study, recreation, and association with friends.

IV. Study in an atmosphere free from distractions. Discipline yourself to total concentration. If you become too tired to continue your study, or if your mind begins to wander, relax for a few minutes before beginning again. Your study period will usually be more worthwhile if you study different subjects for short periods of time rather than sitting down to "study history," for example, for a whole evening. It is possible for you to look at a history book for an entire evening, but it is questionable how much actual study would take place during that time.

V. As you read, jot down words you should look up. (Don't interrupt your reading, however, to look them up.) Also, make a note of quotations and important ideas and dates which are difficult to remember.

CHECK LIST

1. Use of the index is one of the first study skills taught.
2. The dictionary is the most basic reference book. It is really the foundation for all of the others.
3. Students learn to use the encyclopedia, the almanac, and similar references independently.
4. The notebook is an aid to study.

5. Taking notes has both immediate and future value.
6. Outlining skills and other organizational skills promote clear and logical thought.
7. Students must be taught *how* to study.

4

Teaching Spelling
Step by Step

Learning to spell is a long and difficult task. It is a step-by-step procedure that doesn't just happen. Taken step-by-step, though, the difficulties are not staggering. The complexity of the English language presents many problems for the speller, it is true, but these problems are not insurmountable. If you combine sound methods of teaching spelling with at least some student responsibility, you can expect success in the spelling program.

Let's look at some of the reasons why some students are poor spellers:

1. Below average intelligence.
2. A lack of skill with phonetic sounds or an inability to use such useful information as that found in dictionary pronunciation charts.
3. A lack of reading skills and a lack of individual reading. (There are many indications that reading skills and spelling skills progress at much the same rate.)

4. Lack of student interest in improvement of spelling skills.
5. Lack of teacher concern and interest in the student's spelling progress. (The "spelling problem" will be advanced to the next grade at the end of the term; perhaps that teacher will have a solution for him. Too, there is always the possibility of summer school. Too often these seem to be the attitudes taken by some teachers.)

Now, let's look at a short outline for improvement of spelling:

1. Concentration on one spelling problem at a time is a necessary procedure.
2. The teacher and student analyze spelling problems.
3. The alert student keeps some type of record of words which he has misspelled, in an attempt to avoid repetition of the same mistake.
4. Spelling is considered an important skill in all areas of the curriculum.
5. The entire curriculum is designed to help students assume part of the responsibility for learning.

The compensations for faultless spelling are many. First there is the pride and the sense of accomplishment which comes from such an achievement. Then there is the most important result: the ability to express ourselves in a manner which can be understood, especially in writing. There are also the future values of being able to write letters which communicate (a single misspelled word can destroy the effect of an otherwise good letter); of avoiding sometimes stringent penalties on high school and college papers for a single misspelling; of eventually being a responsible employee in a situation which requires spelling skill. (All professional jobs, as well as many others, require well-developed spelling skills.)

SPELLING AND WHAT IT INCLUDES

Learning to spell includes far more than merely placing the letters in correct order. The following is a list of some of the most important skills which are taught in the spelling class:

1. Consonant and vowel sounds
2. Diacritical marks
3. Pronunciation
4. Syllabication
5. Adding prefixes and suffices
6. Forming new words from a root
7. Using words with a hyphen correctly
8. Using words with an apostrophe
9. Using compound words

SPELLING IN AN ORGANIZED CURRICULUM

Spelling in the Lower Grades

In most cases, students first come into contact with spelling in the first grade. The name tag and learning to spell his own name correctly often constitute his first spelling experience. He has for some time seen words displayed in blazing letters on highway billboards and he has seen hundreds of them written across the television screen, and soon after coming to school he may recognize such words as *milk* and *dog* as the teacher writes them or as they are found on displays in the room. He has a curiosity for words and that is the first step toward learning to spell.

In the first grade, the student sees many words written. Often the class, as individuals or as a group, will dictate short stories or experiences to the teacher who will record them. Over and over the child sees the same words written:

pet, cat, dog, mother, father. In this way, he is learning things about words which will help him when he is well enough equipped to actually begin to write words independently.

His first actual written spelling experience usually occurs when he copies, from the teacher's example, a short note to a parent or the title to a picture he has drawn. His first sample of writing will be much less than artistic and it may hardly be decipherable, but for the first grade child, this is a momentous occasion. He has begun to communicate with his pencil.

Specific spelling training actually begins in the second grade. However, a lot of the spelling practice will still be in the form of copied work. In writing a story, a second grade child may ask the teacher for the spelling of many words and these the teacher will write on the board or in some other place. Charts of new words to spell are often used for student reference. Each time someone asks for the spelling of a new word, it is recorded on the chart. After the initial spelling, if the child does not remember how to spell the word, he refers to the chart.

It is also helpful at this level for students to have their own personal word books. They should be as simple as possible with a single letter of the alphabet at the top of each page. As a new word is encountered, the teacher writes the word in the booklet for the student or lets him copy it from the board. Work with simple dictionaries, glossaries, etc., has a part in teaching second graders to spell also.

Spelling in the third grade will take on a somewhat different aspect from that in the second grade. More work with a textbook, dictated lists of words, and learning new spelling skills such as adding simple prefixes and suffixes will take place in third grade. Because some third grade students have more ability to work independently than students in the lower grades, differences in spelling abilities may become more pronounced, requiring detection and more help with individual spelling problems.

Spelling in the Intermediate Grades

In the intermediate grades, spelling should be considered in every subject area. The intermediate student should be encouraged to correct his misspelled words, by using the dictionary and other means available to him. Many intermediate students find that keeping a record of words misspelled is helpful in spelling improvement. This record, though, whether in the form of a notebook, list, or word dictionary, is the responsibility of the individual student. If he does not accept this responsibility, little can be gained by requiring it. At any rate, the teacher's list of misspelled words is extremely important for both the teacher and the student. The list, however, is most effective if it is developed by the entire class adding words as they are missed. The intermediate list should be constructed according to categories:

adding letters
substituting letters
silent letter omitted
failure to double the final consonant
s instead of *c* (and vice versa)
obsolete spelling
no hyphen
no capital letter
wrong prefix or suffix

The spelling class in the intermediate grades is usually a fifteen to twenty minute class conducted five days a week. The materials vary from class to class. Some teachers rely strictly on a textbook series. Others rely almost entirely on class-made lists of words taken from student writing. The third group, usually considered most effective, is the one in which both a text and a class-made list is used.

Textbook series vary a great deal and often a comparison reveals several almost entirely different lists of words, all for the same grade level. Also, it is almost impossible for any list of words to meet the needs of the entire class. Because of these facts, the most effective spelling training can be carried out if the class list of words is also used. If the words have been used in writing by the students, then they are obviously of value to them and should be learned.

The textbook list of weekly words usually includes fifteen to twenty. These words are taught very frequently by the pretest, study, test method. This method usually serves the child's interests better than any other method, as he and the teacher know at the outset of the lesson which words will require the most study. The simpler study, test method assumes that all of the students have a need to study exactly the same words. During the week, the textbook exercises are considered as the teacher feels they have value for the student, in part of the study time. To save time, to increase the rate of speed at which some students work, and to add variety to the class, record words or use the recordings which may accompany your text for the pretest and in some cases for the final test. If possible, it is best to use a recording by a different person than yourself, as hearing a different voice and method of giving the test helps to make the students sharper listeners.

A Spelling Class for Junior High?

Everyone agrees that spelling is an indispensable part of the curriculum for grades one through six, but spelling is often given little attention in junior high. Such a failure is a weakness in the curriculum. A spelling period of at least ten minutes per day should be conducted in the junior high school. Because the words are more difficult at this level, the studies of spelling and vocabulary can be combined most effectively. Unless a student knows the meaning of a word, there is no point in learning to spell it. In a situation where spelling is omitted in junior high, the elementary teachers can share part of the responsibility by determining how effective the incidental spelling training is. It is important that elementary teachers maintain close contact with the junior high language arts teachers to be better able to prepare elementary students for junior high.

LEARNING TO SPELL

Learning to spell is a step-by-step process, and if each step is learned well, progression in spelling will be much simpler. Learning the principal sounds of individual letters, and the sound variations of those same letters, learning the letter combinations which produce specific vowel and consonant sounds, and learning the rules which govern these skills are only a few of the steps which lead to good spelling.

Play by the Rules (Spelling rules are seldom introduced until the intermediate grades.)

Should we use EI or IE? Should the final letter be doubled as in *occurred* or left single as in *kidnaped?* Is G or GUE; C, CH, or CK; PH or GH; EAU, O, OA, or OU; OE, U, or EU correct? Is the plural formed by adding S or by changing the Y to I and adding ES? There are rules which can be followed in making a decision on most of these questions—rules which should be used by the elementary student. Too many spelling rules, unless the student has a definite need for them, are boring and the result is often negligible.

Spelling rules should be introduced and studied as a part of the spelling class *only* if they apply to a large enough group of words to make them worthwhile. For instance, the old rule to "Use I before E except after C, except in *neighbor* and *weigh*" is still indispensable in the spelling class, but this rule should be introduced when the teacher becomes aware that students are having difficulty spelling IE and EI words.

Another rule, that of changing the final Y to I when

it is preceded by a consonant, when adding a suffix, as in *carried,* applies to a sufficiently large number of words to warrant its inclusion in the spelling program. Similarly, other rules should be introduced such as: When a word ends with a C, add a K before adding ING, as in *picnicking;* if the final consonant of a word is preceded by a single vowel, double the final consonant before adding a suffix, as in· *trapping;* when adding a suffix to a word, drop the final silent E unless it is preceded by E or G.

It is easy to see, though, that these rules can be extremely confusing. Requiring students to memorize large numbers of rules can be catastrophic to the spelling program. The rules are very often so complicated that only a good reader can really understand them. But, creative teachers can provide for the learning of those rules which are indispensable to good spelling without bringing boredom to the classroom.

One means of making the study of spelling rules more effective is to choose one rule per week, on the basis of the spelling performance of the students during the week, and display it, in as simple language as possible, in an attractive bulletin board setting. As the week progresses, in addition to the spelling text lesson, the class list of words, and individual spelling problems, the class concentrates on spelling words which depend on use of the rule. The rule should not be overstressed, but as attention is drawn to a misspelling of a word to which the rule applies, the student can quickly refer to the bulletin board. Each week, as the study of a different rule is completed, it should be added to the class list of rules for future reference.

Most spelling rules in the English language have numerous exceptions, and while these need not be overemphasized, they must be included in the study of each rule. No attempt should be made to have the class memorize lists of these exceptions, however. Through use, most students will eventually remember the important exceptions. Notable exceptions such as *seize* and *neither* (exceptions to the IE rule), and *galloping* and *kidnaping* (exceptions to the doubling of final consonant rule) should be considered.

SPECIAL PROBLEMS FOR THE SPELLER

There are many types of problems which confront the spelling student. These problems are far too important to be ignored. The procedure for attacking these problems is most effective if it follows the same pattern used for learning the spelling rules. The spelling problems considered here fit more into the category of exceptions than rules, but they concern a great number of words.

ISE, IZE, or YZE?

Determining the correct word ending is a major spelling difficulty. How many times have you been asked "Is *paralyze* spelled with IZE or YZE? The problem is not really so difficult. Of these three suffixes, the most common is IZE. If you are uncertain of the correct ending, the most logical choice is IZE. There are several hundred words which use this ending. YZE is used in only two common words, *paralyze* and *analyze*. Some of the ordinary words with the ISE ending are merchandISE, despISE, wISE, and exercISE. In most words, all three endings have the identical sound.

CEDE, CEED, or SEDE?

Of these three endings, all of which produce the same sound, CEDE is first in importance, CEED is second, and SEDE is third in use. There is only one common word, *supersede*, which has the SEDE ending. *Proceed, succeed,* and *exceed* are the only common words which use CEED. (CEED is changed to CED in the noun form *procedure*.) All other common words with this sound end with CEDE.

EL, LE, AL, ILE, or IL?

Choosing the correct one of these five common word endings is often difficult because in many cases the sound is identical— (əl). As you study the following lists, you will notice that no rules govern your choice. In most cases the spelling for these words must be memorized. Lists such as these may be compiled in the classroom, if the words have been misspelled in a "use" situation. Of these endings, LE is the most common.

EL	LE	AL	ILE	IL
nickel	brittle	oral	hostile	utensil
cancel	pickle	bridal	missile	nostril
quarrel	wrestle	oval	fragile	tonsil
kernel	valuable	pedal	docile	pencil
caramel	candle	casual	tactile	stencil
model	bridle	rehearsal		
label	muscle	vocal		
parcel	bugle	rascal		
apparel	feeble	medical		
morsel	hustle	legal		

LY or LEY?

LY is a very common suffix which usually means per or like. It can be attached to many words in the language. LEY has a different use and it is used much less frequently. LEY usually forms a part of a basic word. It is not classified as a suffix.

LY	LEY
quickly	barley
lively	trolley
regularly	alley
amply	medley

DOUBLE LETTERS

AArdvark, AArdwolf, bazAAr—these are words which use the double A letter grouping. While these words may not be used in elementary school, the following unique spellings will be, and students should be familiar with them. Because these words and other similar ones are often misspelled, at least one lesson with this type of word in a sixth grade spelling class is necessary.

II——Hawa*ii*, sk*ii*ng
UU——vac*uu*m
LL——*ll*ama
EE——*ee*rie

MORE THAN ONE SPELLING

Another difficulty in spelling is that many words have more than one spelling. It is not uncommon for some texts and other reading materials to inadvertently use the British spelling. This may be a source of confusion for the student unless he realizes that the simpler spelling is almost always the American one and is the acceptable one for use. Also, some dictionaries fail to indicate which spelling is the preferred one. Common examples of these words with which intermediate elementary students should be familiar are:

BRITISH SPELLINGS	AMERICAN SPELLINGS
jewellery	jewelry
colour	color
labour	labor
honour	honor
judgement	judgment
criticise	criticize
benefitted	benefited
cancelled	canceled
travelling	traveling
quarrelled	quarreled
kidnapped	kidnaped
willfully	wilfully

MASCULINE AND FEMININE

It is often necessary, with certain words, to indicate by changing spellings the masculine and the feminine. Elementary students will seldom be asked to do this, but they will encounter these words in their reading. A few examples follow:

MASCULINE	FEMININE
aviator	aviatrix
ambassador	ambassadress
lion	lioness
actor	actress
host	hostess
launderer	laundress

FORMING THE PLURAL WHEN THE FINAL LETTER IS O

Forming plurals causes many difficulties for elementary students. Forming the plural of words whose final letter is O is sometimes especially difficult. Here is a short list which might be compiled during a lesson with plurals:

WITH S	WITH ES	WITH S OR ES OR I
broncos	tomatoes	buffalos or buffaloes
silos	potatoes	mosquitos or mosquitoes
altos	torpedoes	tornados or tornadoes
banjos	mulattoes	sopranos or soprani
portfolios	heroes	solos or soli
studios		volcanos or volcanoes
folios		tobaccos or tobaccoes
rodeos		mementos or mementoes

THE HYPHEN

The following is one example of lesson material which should be part of the intermediate spelling curriculum. Correct use of the hyphen is an important facet of spelling. Your students should be familiar with the following rules which govern the use of the hyphen.

1. Don't divide proper nouns.
2. When combining two words which are not commonly placed together, use the hyphen.

   able-bodied   about-face   absent-minded
   acid-forming   after-dinner   all-American
3. All compound numbers, such as twenty-six, thirty-seven, and seventy-eight, are hyphenated.
4. The hyphen is used to indicate a certain number of pages. For instance, "4-9" means 4 through 9, while "4, 5, 9," means just the numbers 4 and 5 and 9.
5. In some cases, three or more consecutive words may be hyphenated.

   merry-go-round   jack-of-all-trades
6. The hyphen is usually used when *all or like* form part of the compound.

Some compound words can be written either with or without a hyphen. The way it is written depends on the use of the word.

air line   (scheduled air transport——noun)
air-line   (straight as a line in the air——adjective)
ice skate   (the skate itself——noun)
ice-skate   (to skate on ice——verb)

To test your students' knowledge of words of this type, give them several of the following words and let them determine whether the word employs a hyphen, the words are connected without a hyphen, the words are separate, or if the words may be written in more than one way.

HYPHENATED	COMPOUND
letter-perfect	alongshore
life-size	icecap
by-product	alongside
able-bodied	altarpiece
ice-cold	lifetime
Anglo-Indian	bylaw
all-around	letterpress
all-American	fivefold

	WITH OR WITHOUT A
SEPARATE	HYPHEN
life span	about face, about-face
five hundred	ice skate, ice-skate
absolute zero	air line, air-line
ice cap	air mail, air-mail
all right	
all fours	
ice cream	
air alert	

OTHER DIFFICULT SPELLINGS

These difficult spellings are listed here to help you categorize misspellings. Such a categorization helps the student to see order in the spelling process.

SILENT LETTERS Words with silent letters are often difficult to spell. A list of words which fit into this category follows:

aisle	biscuit
salmon	gnaw

WORDS WITH A SINGLE SET OF DOUBLE LETTERS It is often difficult to determine if a word should have a single set of double letters, no double letters, or more than one set of double letters. Here is a list of words with a single set of double letters:

moccasin	vanilla
occasional	tobacco
kangaroo	business

ONE OR TWO Z'S? These six words often give elementary students trouble:

liZard	wiZard	haZard
bliZZard	giZZard	buZZard

WORDS WITH TWO PAIRS OF DOUBLE LETTERS

successful   unnecessary
embarrassed   occurred

WORDS WITH TWO PAIRS OF THE SAME DOUBLE LETTERS

assassin   possess
assess

WORDS WITH THREE SETS OF DOUBLE LETTERS

Mississippi   committee
successfully

LEARN THAT WORD

Spelling with the Tape Recorder

Rather than spending valuable class time dictating spelling words, take advantage of the tape recorder. Record words in groups of ten. The several groups of words recorded should have varying degrees of difficulty in an attempt to meet the needs of the entire class. With the words recorded on the tape recorder, students spell the words until they have mastered them, independently. If you have space and equipment available, several students of the same ability level can utilize the recorder at the same time.

Using the Dictionary

A good habit for students to acquire is that of looking up any word, the spelling of which they are uncertain. Verifying the spelling of a word with a dictionary, however, requires special skill. The student must have a good enough knowledge of spelling that he is aware of more than one possibility for the spelling of a word. Students should have a pocket edition of a standard dictionary at their fingertips almost constantly. Nothing else will improve their spelling as rapidly or as surely.

Detecting a Misspelled Word

Exercises such as the following can help students detect misspelled words. First they locate the misspelled word/ words and then they correct it:

1. He was at the botom of the pile.
2. The letter A is a vowell.
3. Try to prononce the word correctly.
4. He excaped silently.
5. The duke spoke to the lady politly.
6. Last night we watched a new television program on chanel 5.
7. The wrestler was very sucessful in the ring.
8. L is the nineth consonant in the alphabet.

SUCCESS OR FAILURE?

Evaluation of spelling should include far more than grading a single weekly list of textbook words. Many students are able to memorize a list of rather difficult words and spell them perfectly when they are dictated, but a short time later they are misspelling the words in a writing situation. This brings us to the conclusion that memorized words are not necessarily learned words. Words must be used by most students many times before they actually become a part of their learned words.

The evaluation of spelling words is more effective if the list of words is given in the setting of a short and interesting paragraph or story. One means of doing this is for the teacher to read the paragraph slowly, allowing enough time for writing the words but not time for tedious thought and multiple changes. Other teachers prefer to give a grade on spelling performance in creative writing, because in a creative writing situation, the student's mind is more on content than on mechanical skills and because of this the teacher has a better indication of his spelling ability.

The teacher should keep a list of words during the week, from all of the subject areas, if possible, and include part of these on the week's evaluation list. If five or more students have misspelled the same word, it should become a part of the list. (Some teachers include a word if only three have misspelled it.) These words are the ones which should receive the most attention. They should become part of a year-long list of difficult words. In some situations, to avoid an unmanageably long list of words, the teacher may have to limit the weekly list to five or ten words. Several times during the year the words are reviewed. Misspelled words which are obviously results of carelessness should not be included on the list. The list that follows is one example from a class of twenty students.

WORD MISSPELLED	NUMBER MISSING WORD	TYPE OF ERROR
1. error	9	airer, arrer, arower, aerer, erer, arror
2. tongue	6	tonuge, tungh, tonge, toung
3. border	8	boarder, borador, bourder, bordor
4. woolen	3	wolen, woollen, woolan
5. wrestle	12	restle, rasle, wrisel, resectle, ressal, recile
6. similar	11	simalar, simular, simler, simalor, similier
7. valuable	7	valouble, valueable, valuble

8. groceries	5	grocorys, gorcires, greoceries, grosaries
9. incorrect	8	incorret, incerect, incollect, incorect, encorrect
10. strength	9	strengt, strenth, stenth, strinkth, strenith, strinked

CHECK LIST

1. The teacher must consider the various reasons for poor spelling.
2. Each phase of spelling must first be considered separately, then together, so that the several aspects of spelling form a unified whole.
3. A good foundation in spelling can be built by teaching the various skills step by step and grade by grade.
4. Spelling is a skill which requires much practice.
5. The spelling class should be extended into Junior High School.
6. Students must learn the rules for spelling as well as the exceptions which so often become the rule.
7. Spelling problems are to be considered individually.
8. Evaluating students' spelling is one of the most important aspects of spelling.

5

Creating an Interest
in Words

A well-organized vocabulary program is one which stimulates interest in words by providing meaningful motivation and instruction while at the same time providing for and encouraging independent discovery. The well-organized program recognizes the limited or "controlled" amount of new words in many of the basic texts, and supplies other books and reading materials to compensate for a lack in this area. The well-planned program, if it is to benefit the student, stresses the knowledge of words for use rather than merely for the sake of knowledge.

We consider vocabulary at this point because so much of the curriculum depends on a good knowledge of words. At the same time, we must recognize that in most cases vocabulary is taught as a part of other subject areas, rather than as a separate entity. In the early primary grades we are concerned with teaching a good basic vocabulary, a vocabulary which will provide the key to reading with understanding, and a vocabulary which will provide the means for correct and meaningful oral communication. A limited number of specialized vocabulary words are introduced in the lower grades.

During the intermediate grades, mastery of each subject area depends on the knowledge of a specialized vocabulary. By the end of sixth grade, for instance, a social studies student is expected to know words like politics, industry, democracy, latitude, longitude, culture, etc. In literature, he will have been exposed to such terms as novel, antagonist, protagonist, flashback, metaphor.

The greatest addition of new vocabulary seems to have come in the areas of mathematics and science. It is not at all uncommon for intermediate science students to be exposed to these rather difficult words: ecology, bacteriologist, biochemistry, ethology, hormone, and microbe. Finally, in mathematics, the vocabulary is even more specialized. Terms which until a few years ago mathematics students didn't encounter until the high school years have reached all the way down to the first and second grades. It is understandable, then, that many students, teachers, and parents are, at first contact with these terms, not a little disgruntled: binary operation, line segment, one-to-one correspondence, and quadrilateral.

Can we afford to fail in teaching students a good vocabulary? Can we teach vocabulary effectively only in the subject areas other than language arts? What word attack skills and what keys to understanding words should be learned in the elementary grades? Which approaches are most effective? These questions provide the basis for this chapter.

CREATING AN INTEREST IN WORDS

Our first objective in teaching vocabulary is to stimulate an interest in words. If this can be done through word games, colorful bulletin board displays and other creative devices originated by the teacher, some of the students will soon be searching for new words and their meanings independently. Many others will be curious enough, when a new word is encountered, to look for its meaning in a dictionary.

Too often a child's ability with words is underestimated. This type of situation can cause boredom and lack of learning just as too difficult words can.

Independent Discovery

Let students discover as much about words as possible by themselves. Don't dampen interest by giving them complete lists "to study." Occasionally, students might develop their own lists and a master list might be compiled as a group project and distributed to the entire class. But students like to make discoveries independently. Much more benefit is derived from a situation in which a student discovers that hydrogen, hydra, and hydro-electric are related in meaning, than in a situation in which the teacher draws this conclusion for the student.

Words on Exhibit

USING THE BLACKBOARD One means of stimulating interest in words is to place one or more interesting words on a section of the blackboard each day for individual study or for class discussion. But be certain the words used meet the following standards:

1. Words are within students' ability level.
2. Words have enough interest that students will read them independently.
3. The structure of the words provides keys to the meaning of other words.

Here are examples of words which have been used in successful classroom situations:

OUTLANDISH: Our attention was detracted from the speaker by the lady's *outlandish* hat. (Draw students' attention to the fact that *outlandish* originally meant foreign but it now means extremely extraordinary.)

HERBIVOROUS: an animal which feeds on grasses and herbs is *herbivorous*. A horse is a *herbivorous* animal.

RIVERINE: living in or near a river. A hippopotamus is a *riverine* animal.

TAXIDERMIST: taxis (arrangement); derm (skin); -ist (skilled in); the art of preserving animals and animal skins for display. The taxidermist mounted the huge polar bear for the museum.

Other words used for motivation might be *dodo, eke, hydra, llama,* and *dromedary.*

BULLETIN BOARD   Many bulletin board displays can be used in the classroom to teach new words and to reinforce those learned previously. Here are a few bulletin board examples which can be used with success in the elementary classroom.

I.   "New Words Are Born": Under this topic, some of the many new words in science, especially in the area of space, are used with colorful and descriptive illustrations.

II.   "Keys to Word Meanings": A display of word prefixes and suffixes which are pertinent to some area of current study is made. Various techniques can be used to fix these word elements firmly in the student's mind. Let's take the example of AQUA-. The following list of words and appropriate illustrations can be used to make an entire display. (Since the prefix AQUA- is the one under study, it should be in prominent letters each time it appears in a word.)

AQUArium
AQUAnaut
AQUEduct
AQUAplane
AQUArius   (One or two students may write a re-

port on Aquarius, "the water bearer," accompanied by the zodiacal sign, for the display.)

III. Similarly, here is an outline for a display using other prefixes:

SUB-	SUBmarine	(appropriate pictures and illustrations)
TRANS-	TRANSoceanic	(appropriate pictures and illustrations)
SUPER-	SUPERsonic	(appropriate pictures and illustrations)

IV. Other displays may be more closely associated with a special topic being studied. In science, a sixth grade study of oceanography may call for keyed diagrams of the ocean. Such a display makes specialized vocabulary meaningful.

WORD WHEEL A word wheel, similar to the one pictured, is a motivational device for presenting word patterns and words of interest. The words should be changed regularly. Students might be encouraged to take the initiative and after discovering new word patterns, present them to the class through this medium. AQUA-, RE-, MIS-, and SUB-, are other examples which might be used on the word wheel. Words relating to a particular field of interest, but having different derivations, can also be used successfully.

Word Games

Word games often help students in learning new vocabulary words. Responses should be kept on a voluntary basis, however. But before you suggest any word game, be certain it will be of some immediate value to the students. Your list of standards might include the following:

1. The game presents new and meaningful words and helps students understand them.
2. It helps to form good speech habits.

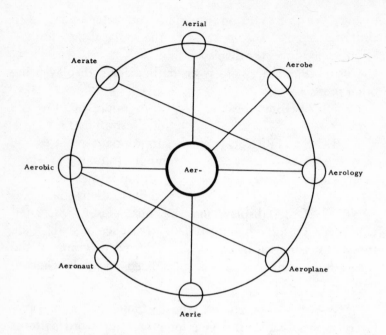

3. It helps to teach courtesy.

Many variations of the following game can serve as learning devices. Each student chooses an occupation, then the game proceeds as follows:

1ST STUDENT: I am a selenologist, what do I do?
RESPONSE: You study the moon—its surface, the possibilities of life there, etc.
2ND STUDENT: I am an architect. Can you describe my work?—etc.

CONTEXT CLUES   Another word game is this one which gives students practice with context clues. Here is an example. Students fill in the blanks as the story is read orally. (Each teacher can easily adapt it to his classroom rules.)

A_____is an animal usually found in polar _____. It has a large thick neck and a rather long, bulky body. It has no feet but it is able to

swim with its_____which resemble paddles.
It has a gray or brown_____. It lives, eats,
and sleeps, most of the time, in_____. Its favorite food is_____. Sometimes it_____
thousands of miles to join its own group. One
of the uses man makes of the_____ is
_____. . . .

MATCHING GAME   Students have fun and learn from a
matching game with group words such as the following:

1. A gaggle of	(geese)
2. A flock of	(birds)
3. A pack of	(wolves)
4. A herd of	(elephants)
5. A school of	(fish)
6. A covey of	(quail)
7. A pride of	(lions)
8. A pod of	(whales)
9. An army of	(ants)
10. A brood of	(chickens)

(Some of the above have more than one answer.)

ASSOCIATION GAMES   In this game students are given
words and asked to assign them to a particular field. For
instance: assign such words as the list of words on the left to
one of the fields on the right. (Should be played orally.)

vitamin	science
fraction	math
olé	social studies
synagogue	language
election	religion
hibernation	
Latin	

The same game can be used as a study or review of place
names or some other similar study. Here is an example:

MATCH THE FOLLOWING:

Kenya	mountain
Leningrad	country
Caspian	state
Suez	city
Gobi	island
Euphrates	canal
Grand Coulee	river
Golden Gate	continent
Huron	lake
Carlsbad	sea
Europe	ocean
Atlantic	desert
Taiwan	dam
Everest	cave
Maine	bridge

The same game may be played with people and their areas of work: Einstein, scientist; Frost, poet; Lincoln, president. Games such as these acquaint students with new words and because working with words in ways such as these is fun, they often remember them longer. They are games which can, with modifications in the lists of words, be played at any grade level. They may be played in language arts class at any grade level or adapted to other subject areas.

REVERSIBLE WORDS   As a different approach to vocabulary study, students can find words which can be reversed to form new words. The following is a typical list:

ward	draw
leer	reel
leek	keel
dual	laud
loot	tool
loop	pool
reed	deer
dial	laid

tub	but
gas	sag

An extension of this exercise is to find words which, when reversed, are the same:

gag	eye
pop	wow
tot	bob
eke	mum
eve	nun
ewe	

RHYMING WORDS   To vary the word study, the following approach may be used. This is a means of acquainting students with unique words which will enhance their vocabularies. It also gives them a better idea of how words are born. Much of the work in this area will be independent.

hurdy-gurdy	a barrel organ
hurly-burly	an uproar
hurry-scurry	hurried confusion
hula-hula	a Hawaiian dance
pell-mell	confused haste
hari-kari	Japanese ritual suicide
hodgepodge	a jumbled mixture
agar-agar	an extract of seaweed
higgledy-piggledy	jumbled disorder
hi-fi	high fidelity

HOW ARE WORDS LEARNED?

A fourth grade student in reading an assigned lesson on forestry in social studies may encounter these new words: *Forestation, lumberjack, humus, tropical, commercial.* If he is a particularly bright child, he will probably be able to remember most of the words and their meanings without rereading or reviewing the lesson. If he has the skills of an average reader, he will be able to understand the explanations and illustrations given. If he is a slow student, these words will be difficult ones for him.

The bright child will be challenged by these words and perhaps he will do considerable follow-up reading on the subject of forestation. The average child can learn and remember the words if he reviews them sufficiently. The slow student who sees these words as difficult will not learn the words unless many visual aids are provided, he hears the words used several times, and he himself uses the words. Even then, he may not remember them. Often the slow child seems to view such situations as the above lesson as hopeless.

In too many classes, where there are students of every ability level, new words are introduced to them day after day, and students lacking word attack skills, self-motivation, and teacher motivation fail to learn the new words. Soon the student is floundering in an unfamiliar morass of new words and concepts which he is unable to grasp. He is pushed from class to class and grade to grade for more non-learning.

In a situation where such shoddy training in vocabulary exists, the problem is compounded. If he cannot understand the words—by learning them thoroughly as they are presented, or developing word attack skills which can help him determine word meanings—he may be a failure throughout his school years.

Let's look at the five new words again:

Forestation and lumberjack: Most fourth grade students will have little difficulty with these words. Most can readily see that here, a single word, *forestation,* takes the place of several other words—planting trees to cover an area—or *lumberjack*—one who cuts down trees in a forest. Here, students are still on fairly familiar ground. The concrete words *forest* and *lumber* are familiar ones even to second graders. Learning these words, then, is primarily a matter of attaching a new concept to old words.

Humus: Don't underestimate the importance of first-hand experience throughout the elementary grades. Humus is an entirely new word to most fourth graders. Since it does involve a new concept, the best possible way to teach the word is by first-hand experience. Bring a sample of humus to the classroom for examination.

Tropical: With the use of maps, globes, and other visual aids, students can understand this rather concrete adjective with little difficulty.

Commercial: This word will undoubtedly cause the most difficulty.

PROCEDURE

Read as a class, the sentence in which the word appeared: It might have been "Our northwestern states have many *commercial* forests."

Gather the following information:

Commercial licenses: (used on vehicles used by businessmen)

Not for *commercial* use: (samples are not to be sold)

Chamber of *commerce:* (an organization of businessmen)

Advertising: (This *commercial* paid for by. . . .)

The class then draws the conclusion that COMMERCIAL relates to business and refers to something which is to be sold for profit.

Word Patterns

Children are intrigued with sound patterns, whether those patterns are in poetry, songs, nursery rhymes, or just in everyday speech. Capitalize on student interest in sound and word patterns. A large percentage of our words can be categorized according to a pattern. Patterns can help establish association necessary for learning.

It is often helpful to categorize a number of words which

have similar suffixes, prefixes, or word origins, when learning a new related word. For instance, when the word *pedestrian* is encountered, the following related words will help some students understand its meaning.

PEDal   centiPEDE
biPED   milliPEDE

After students have examined these words and their meanings they will have little difficulty understanding that PED- often means foot.

The same procedure can successfully be followed with these sets of words:

FloridIAN   machinIST   bioLOGY
PanamanIAN   specialIST   geoLOGY
OregonIAN   dentIST   zoöLOGY
barbarIAN   typIST

It is almost of no value to give students lists such as these unless they are to be used to help students understand or to reinforce the meaning of a similar patterned word. In such a case, a brief list is not a curse to the student, but a tool.

Related Words

Lists of vocabulary words do create inhibitions in the classroom if they have no purpose and if they are overused. To the student, unrelated vocabulary lists mean dull hours with a dictionary, tedious hours of memorization, and finally a frustrating evaluation. Even if the student has expended a great deal of effort, often no measurable accomplishment in word understanding has resulted. But, the presentation of a group of related words to the students often provides a valuable learning experience. A carefully constructed list can motivate students to further study in a particular field of interest. Words should follow a natural progression from simple to more difficult words, however. The similarity of the words will help create an organized thought pattern so vitally important in learning. In the study of various units, lists similar to the following might be compiled:

SLAVERY	COAL	POPULATION
overseer	vein	rural
abolish	shaft	urban
emancipate	ore	suburban
quadroon	peat	urbane
mulatto	lignite	metropolitan
plantation	anthracite	cosmopolitan

Some Keys to Words

In helping students build a good vocabulary, it is necessary to avoid excessive drill. Admittedly, a certain amount of "drill" is helpful if it is properly directed. A few of the prefixes, suffixes and other word elements which are basic in building a good vocabulary are often not included in traditional textbooks and must be gotten from another source by the teacher. Many of these prefixes and other word elements should be learned by the student. The following ten prefixes of Latin origin are the keys to many numerical terms. Because of the wide use of word elements such as these, as well as of those included in other similar tables, these tables are important in teaching vocabulary.

PREFIX	VALUE		USE
mille	1000	million	1 plus 6 zeros
bi	2	billion	1 plus 9 zeros
tri	3	trillion	1 plus 12 zeros
quad	4	quadrillion	1 plus 15 zeros
quint	5	quintillion	1 plus 18 zeros
sex	6	sextillion	1 plus 21 zeros
sept	7	septillion	1 plus 24 zeros
oct	8	octillion	1 plus 27 zeros
non	9	nonillion	1 plus 30 zeros
deci	10	decillion	1 plus 33 zeros

The following table also provides the key to so many words in the English language that its importance cannot be overlooked.

PREFIX	MEANING	WORD USE
aqua	water	aquanaut
bene	good	benefit
fin	end	finish
magni	great	magnify
mal	bad	malevolent
multi	many	multimillionaire
neg	to deny	negate
pater	father	paternal
mater	mother	maternal
vita	life	vitamin
terra	earth	terrarium
mare	sea	maritime
urbs	city	urban
oculus	eye	oculist
canis	dog	canine

If words are to be learned well, words must not be taught as separate entities, but as a part of a unified structure, dependent on key suffixes, prefixes, and other basic word elements. Taught in this way, vocabulary begins to have meaning for the student in all subject areas.

Root Words

Students in the lower grades can begin to understand root words and word formation through words with which they are familiar. If students learn the root words well, they will soon be able to understand longer words based on the root. Learning of the suffixes and prefixes of these words often is most effective through use. An introductory exercise with root words might include the following:

long	length
high	height
wide	width
deep	depth
warm	warmth
solemn	solemnity
miser	miserable
luxury	luxurious
compose	composition
recreate	recreation

Word Story Box

A "Word Story Box" is an interesting teaching device for the classroom. As new words with interesting histories are learned, students write a short story about the word and place it in the box. Students not only learn while finding and recording these word histories, but the box is a handy reference source for the classroom. Here are examples of words which might be used in an elementary classroom:

Ballot: The instrument of secret voting was originally a little ball. Various systems were used, but the most common was that of dropping a white ball in the box for yes and a black ball in the box for no. (Black meant no, hence "blackballing.")

Canoe: This word originally meant twice across the ocean.

Quarantine: At one time, ships on which there was a contagious disease were held in port for *forty* days under all circumstances. The length of time was later an arbitrary matter, but the meaning remained much the same.

The Vocabulary Notebook

Keeping a vocabulary notebook can be an effective way to learn new words. This activity may begin quite early in the primary grades. Students should be encouraged to be responsible for keeping their notebooks up to date— adding words regularly. They can set their own goals for the notebook. It might be one or two words per day. The major source for these words should be individual reading. Encourage them to keep a scratch pad on their desks on which to record new words as they read. Suggest that they look up words in a dictionary only after they have finished reading. Such interruptions slow one's reading speed, and it is important that they determine the meaning of the word through context.

PRACTICE WITH WORDS

Important Words in Poetry

Finding the action words in a short, interesting poem is one way of teaching students which words are most important in a sentence. Another activity with poetry is that of finding the words which have been written to create a picture in the mind of the reader. Let's look at an example.

In the poem "The Fawn" by Edna St. Vincent Millay, students might underline such words as *monstrous, beautiful, spotty,* and *plain.* An interesting follow-up for this activity is that of comparing mental pictures created by the poem.

Homonyms: End the Confusion

There are many areas of our language which are confusing. Special practice in these areas, though, can help to end the confusion. Homonyms are often trouble-makers for the students. Some common homonyms which are used frequently in the elementary school are:

bury	berry
bass	base
canvas	canvass

board	bored
bold	bowled
seen	scene
air	heir
tie	Thai
capital	Capitol
principal	principle

The following is an exercise designed to give students practice with homonyms:

1. The (reining, raining, reigning) king was removed from his (throne, thrown) during the revolution.
2. Bob (pride, pried) up the garage window with a short (peace, piece) of (wood, would).
3. We spent a (hole, whole) day on the (beach, beech).
4. (Our, hour) trip around the (Straight, Strait) of Magellan was a stormy (one, won).
5. It was very difficult to (toe, tow) the old (sale-, sail-) boat to shore.
6. We (stayed, staid) at the (site, cite, sight) of the accident until the ambulance arrived.
7. Jim's (mussels, muscles) were (sore, soar) after his (assent, ascent) up the (side, sighed) of the mountain.
8. A (waive, wave) capsized the boat.
9. Many (styles, stiles) change during the (course, coarse) of a single year.
10. Our (please, pleas) to the (principle, principal) failed (to, too, two) (alter, altar) his decision.

Words from Other Languages

Many words have been incorporated into the English language from other languages, to which we give the original pronunciation and attach the same meaning. Because of their constant use, elementary students should have a knowledge of them. One of the most effective ways of teaching them is through a bulletin board display. Different words from as many of the major languages as possible are located by the students for the display. This activity helps students understand how much of our language comes from other languages. It also serves to broaden their vocabulary experience. Here are a few of the words which we use frequently:

musicale	a musical party	(French)
esprit de corps	a sense of compatibility	(French)
a cappella	without musical accompaniment	(Italian)
beret	a round flat cap	(French)
chic	stylish	(French)
chop suey	Chinese food	(Chinese)
cliché	a trite expression	(French)
clique	a small select group	(French)
ad-lib	to improvise	(Latin)
à la mode	in fashion	(French)
alma mater	foster mother	(Latin)
adios	good-by	(Spanish)
aloha	a greeting	(Hawaiian)
par excellence	by excellence	(French)
ballet	a dance	(Italian)
bamboo	Malayan tree	(Malayan)

6

Teaching the Proper
Use of Words

Building a good vocabulary can be fun, but it involves a great deal of practice. The practice, however, should be continuous and varied enough to hold the interest of the student.

One of the common error judgments of some elementary teachers is often made in determining difficulty. Very often teachers avoid words which are within the limits of students' understanding because they appear too difficult. For example, the word *hemidemisemiquaver* is a very long word, but students find it interesting, because of its length and uniqueness. The value of teaching this word is that three similar prefixes which are keys to many words can be learned here easily.

Why is vocabulary traning so important? A good vocabulary constitutes the means to intelligible speech, to concise writing, and to reading comprehension. But, we cannot place too much emphasis on the fact that vocabulary training is important in every area of the curriculum and that this training must be consistent. Too, let us reemphasize the importance of short, interesting, and constant vocabulary training. If the teacher can help the student to discover the keys to words, presented in this book, the student will progress much faster and much more smoothly in his search for knowledge.

This section of the book is divided into a series of actual short vocabulary assignments which help form the basis for a thorough understanding of words. Accompanying each assignment is a short explanation of how the vocabulary assignment can benefit the student, and of how it can be presented most effectively.

I. PROPER NOUNS

Proper nouns and proper adjectives are widely used in our language; therefore, they warrant our attention. There are two major points to consider when studying these words.

A. Pronunciation (FLORida—FloRIDian)

B. Spelling (-an or -ian, etc. Italy—Italian)

It is easy to make a game with these words, thus avoiding tiresome drill.

EXERCISE: (ASK ORALLY OR LET STUDENTS QUESTION EACH OTHER)

1. A person from California is a *CALIFORNIAN.*
2. A person from Florida is a *FLORIDIAN.*
3. A person from New York is a *NEW YORKER.*
4. A person from Denmark is a *DANE.*
5. A person from Norway is a *NORWEGIAN.*
6. A person who lives in the suburbs is a *SUBURBANITE.* (The suffix -ITE can be used with many proper nouns, especially cities.)
7. Where is a Venetian from?
8. A person from Japan is a *JAPANESE.* (-ESE is also a common adjective and noun suffix.)

9. A person from Israel is an *ISRAELI*. (Note the I suffix.)
10. A person from Spain is a *SPANIARD*.
11. A man from France is a *FRENCHMAN*.

II. NEGATIVE PREFIXES

Children can enlarge their vocabularies considerably, simply by adding a negative prefix to many words. However, some may have difficulty associating the correct prefix with the right word. Here are a few of the common negative prefixes which elementary children can understand:

a- + social = ASOCIAL;   not social

un- + abridged = UNABRIDGED;   not limited
   This is a word which the teacher can help the children to learn through use. They should understand a reference to "the unabridged dictionary."

non- + sale + able = NONSALABLE;   cannot be sold or is not worth selling

in + able + ity = INABILITY;   does not have the strength to do

im + mature = IMMATURE;   is not mature

ab- + normal = ABNORMAL;   Ninety-five is an ABNORMAL human body temperature.

il- + legal = ILLEGAL;   not legal

ir- + regular = IRREGULAR;   not regular

ig- + noble = IGNOBLE;   not noble—infamous

anti- + freeze = ANTIFREEZE;   a substance to keep a liquid from freezing, usually water

Also with this group of prefixes, there is sometimes a change in pronunciation, as in comPARE—COMparable. Spellings of root woods are often changed too, as in IR-REPARABLE (ir + repair + able).

A short matching exercise such as the following can help to reinforce the students' learning of these prefixes. Choose the correct prefix.

1. pleasant	a. ir
2. existent	b. un
3. appear	c. non
4. slavery	d. de
5. typical	e. ab
6. populate	f. im
7. normal	g. in
8. accurate	h. il
9. responsible	i. dis
10. noble	j. anti
11. legal	k. a
12. polite	l. ig

An extension of this activity is to have students fill in the blanks of exercises such as the following:

1. It is (not polite) to stare at people.
2. It is (not legal) to park on the left side of the street in Elmwood.
3. Some children wear braces to straighten (not regular) teeth.
4. The black shoes are half-price because they are (not perfect).
5. It is (not logical) to look toward the east to watch the sun set.
6. Mrs. Baker waited (without patience) for the rain to stop.
7. Mr. Thompson said he could not hire an (without experience) person.
8. "Bob," Mrs. Vinton said, "your third answer is (not correct)."

III. MORE PREFIXES AND SUFFIXES

More practice with prefixes and suffixes can come through word opposites:

disappear	(reappear)
discourage	(encourage)

disarm   (rearm)
disassociate   (reassociate)

When studying each of these groups of words, encourage students to discover similar words by themselves.

IV. WORDS AND THE DICTIONARY

Dictionary practice can become very boring and have little value if the words are far too simple or too difficult. However, creative students find that new words are full of interest.

Learning new words is like solving puzzles. Discovering one word element may unlock the meaning of a word. Examples can be seen in the following practice exercise:

1. A PENTAD is a period of 5 years. (pen- = 5)
2. A CRANIOLOGIST is a skull expert. (crani- = skull)
3. A PINE is a CONIFEROUS tree. (con- = cone)
4. A DECAPOD has 10 feet. (deca- = 10; pod- = foot)
5. CONTRARY is the root of CONTRARIETY.
6. A NABOB is an Englishman who has become rich in INDIA.
7. A NAVICULAR (navy) bone or object is BOAT shaped.
8. LACUSTRINE (lake) means of or like a LAKE.
9. SLAVOCRACY means_____.

One phase of a good vocabulary is the ability to associate the names of well-known people with a major field of interest. The following exercise is an important one in dictionary usage. *Match the following:*

1. Euclid   a. author
2. Aesop   b. fabulist
3. John Brown   c. social worker
4. Louisa May Alcott   d. inventor

5. Andrew Carnegie	e. liberator
6. Simon Bolivar	f. abolitionist
7. Jane Addams	g. politician
8. Louis Braille	h. mathematician
9. Nicolaus Copernicus	i. industrialist
10. Hernando De Soto	j. scientist
11. William Jennings Bryan	k. explorer

Other Words and Their Meanings

Words which seem very difficult can be introduced. Experiment with the word ABECEDARIAN. Write it in blocked letters in a conspicuous place on the chalk board. Do not draw attention to it. Let the students discover it. Try this experiment for several days. How observant are your students?

After students have discovered the meaning of the difficult word, you may wish to discuss the word, letting a student explain its meaning. Students have fun trying to "stump" the rest of the class with other words such as TRANSNEPTUNIAN (Trans- = across or beyond + Neptune + ian) and RETROCHOIR (retro = behind, going backwards + choir) or HERBIVOROUS (an animal that eats herbs or grasses).

The -OLOGY Words

On the surface, the -OLOGY words may seem difficult to both teachers and students. However, they are much more easily understood than a mere cursory examination of the words may reveal.

The word element -LOGY means study of or science of. To this suffix, we add -IST, which changes a word to a noun. With this knowledge, one needs only to determine the meaning of the first part of the word and the meaning of the word will be clear. Introducing these words is not merely an arbitrary matter. Elementary science students, for instance, even in the lower grades, are confronted with a great many -OLOGY words. In fact, much of their understanding of the sciences depends on learning -OLOGY words and many others of similar difficulty. Here are several examples which can be dealt with by elementary students:

AERology	(air)
ANTHROPology	(man)
ARCHAEology	(ancient man)
BIOlogy	(life)
CHRONology	(time)
EPIDEMIology	(epidemics)
GEOlogy	(earth)
GRAPHology	(writing)
HYDROlogy	(water)
MICROBIOlogy	(miniature organisms)
OÖlogy	(study of bird eggs)
ZOÖlogy	(animals)

Similarities Among Languages

Cognates are words which have much the same meaning and spelling in more than one language. They are derived from the same root and they have retained the original definition. Study the following words and note the similarities:

ENGLISH	poem	minute	number	climate
FRENCH	poeme	minute	numero	climat
SPANISH	poema	minuto	numero	clima
PORTUGUESE	poema	minuto	numero	clima
ITALIAN	poema	minuto	numero	clima

Using a multi-lingual dictionary, students may wish to find more of these cognates.

Word Derivations

Our language has its roots in every major language in the world, but over sixty percent of the words in our language have origins in Latin. Names, whims, and misunderstandings are a few of the many other origins. Many of these words have richly interesting histories which shed considerable light on the anatomy of our language. Students need to understand the origins of at least some of our words. An interesting study of word origins is one way of starting students on a serious search for new words.

PROCEDURE   Give students a list of proper names and ask them to try to determine which common words were derived from them. Occasionally you may wish to reverse the assignment and give them the word first and ask them to determine the origin. A sample list of proper names which can be used for this exercise follows:

Louis PASTEUR:	pasteurization
J. G. ZINN:	the zinnia flower
J. L. McADAM:	the macadam road
AMERICUS Vespucci:	America
Jacques NICOT:	nicotine
Joseph SAC:	the saxophone
Captain BOYCOTT:	boycott (the first victim of a boycott)

PLACE NAMES

The same procedure used in the previous exercise can be used here effectively. Here are some examples for study:

FRANKFORT, Germany:	frankfurter
HAMBURG, Germany:	hamburger
BAYONNE, France:	bayonet
SHETLAND Islands:	Shetland pony

The following categories of place names offer interesting possibilities for study:

Cities from other countries: *Examples*—Florence, Ala. (Italy); New London, Connecticut (England); Lisbon, Maine (Portugal)

Names of other countries: *Examples*—Brazil, Indiana; Mexico, Maine; England, Arkansas

Names of presidents: *Examples*—Jackson, Mississippi; Monroe, New York; Jefferson City, Missouri

Names of famous people: *Examples*—Lafayette, Alabama; Whittier, California; Revere, Massachusetts

Names from natural features: *Examples*—Little Rock, Arkansas; Long Beach, California; Green Bay, Wisconsin

Words from Mythology

Many of our words are taken from mythology. To make your study of mythology interesting and more meaningful, review some of the mythological names which have been used in our language to form words. This exercise should be one of discovery, rather than one of rote learning:

VULCAN	vulcanize
TERRA	terrace
TITAN	titanic
HERCULES	herculean
ATLAS	atlas
CHRONOS	chronology
HYPNOS	hypnosis
OCEANUS	ocean
PAN	panic

How Words Develop

The meanings of words are changing constantly. As old meanings become obsolete, new ones are substituted. A few words for which meanings have changed are included in the following list. Many of our words, however, have the same meanings as when they were originated, but they do have an interesting history.

Salary: This word gets its name from the ancient practice of giving Roman soldiers a part of their pay as a special allowance for salt.

Algebra: The word "algebra" once meant bone setting.

Lunatic: It was once thought that moonshine caused insanity, and since the Latin word for moon is luna, the word lunatic naturally developed.

Students can find many other words with interesting histories to add color to their study of words.

Understanding Prefixes

Teaching students to combine words correctly is a very important oral and written skill which adds to the vocabulary. The following prefixes and words must simply be learned. This can best be done by associating the prefix with a familiar word. The following examples are words and prefixes which are part of the elementary curriculum.

CIRCUM-(around   CIRCUMFERENCE means distance around.

COUNTER-(opposite)   COUNTERCLOCKWISE means from right to left.

INTER- (between or among)   INTERCONTINENTAL means between continents.

INTRA-(within)   INTRASTATE means within a state.

POST-(after)   A POSTSCRIPT is written at the end of a letter.

PRE-(before)   PREHISTORIC means before the events of history were recorded.

ULTRA-(beyond)   ULTRAMONTANE
                       means across or beyond
                       the mountains.

CO-(together)   COOPERATE means to
                       work together.

EX-(from, out)   EXTERIOR means the
                       outside.

Use the Word

To assure understanding of a word, give students an opportunity to use different forms and different meanings of the word. Exercises such as the following teach skills in word use.

FALSE

His efforts to FALSIFY the reports were in vain.
The speaker's first statement was a FALSEHOOD.
The soloist sang several songs in a FALSETTO.

FAMILIAR

Please FAMILIARIZE yourself with the rules, to
   prevent errors.
His FAMILIARITY with many of the government
   officials was a distinct advantage.
The immigrants were UNFAMILIAR with many
   of our customs.

FINAL

The lengthy convention FINALLY came to an end.
The FINALITY of the report discouraged the pro-
   testers.
Jack was a FINALIST in the gold medal competition.

FORMULA

After the experiment, the scientist began to FOR-
MULATE the results.
The FORMULATION of the results of an experi-
ment is extremely important.

EMPLOY

The young graduate was searching for rewarding
EMPLOYMENT.
As an EMPLOYEE, he hoped to use the knowledge
he had gained.
He knew, however, that his EMPLOYER would
establish the rules.

Correct Pronunciation

Being able to pronounce words correctly is such an
important part of vocabulary training that it cannot be ignored. Give your students the dictionary spellings for words
such as the following and ask them to give the English
spelling, then ask them to pronounce the words correctly.

muscle	choir
seize	yacht
gnarl	dachshund
psalm	leopard
exist	receive

CHECK LIST

1. Do students realize the importance of a good vocabulary?
2. Have the students set goals for themselves, to
help build a good vocabulary?
3. How well can they use the dictionary in locating
word origins, etc.?

4. How familiar are they with the actual mechanics of words—prefixes, suffixes, etc.?
5. How adept are they at determining word meanings from various word elements?
6. Have they studied and developed an interest in word histories, how new words are formed, and how word meanings change?
7. Are they using new words they have learned?

7

How to Teach
Creative Writing Techniques

Trends toward more creativity in education have forced
impressive changes in teaching methods as well as in subject content. Interest, color, and individual expression are
recognized as indispensable components. The well-oriented
classroom is no longer a pedagogical wasteland, but rather,
a stimulating atmosphere conducive to learning. A more
positive concept of the teacher has also been developing.
We now conceive of the teacher as not only a teacher, but
also as a supervisor and coordinator, instigating and piloting
the educational program which will develop the student to
his full potential. While every area of the curriculum is
alert to originality, results are evidenced most in the language
arts, particularly in writing.

Since students have been given more freedom in writing
and since experimentation in this area has been encouraged,
student writing has taken a new form. The latitude of topics
permitted ranges from the reproduction process of a para-
mecium to illicit bargaining in a political campaign. But,
what about conforming to the rules of conventional writing?

In increasingly more classrooms, the teacher's initial concern is with what the student writes rather than with how he writes it. He is also concerned with the child's improvement. And this, of course, should be determined, not by the teacher's standards, not by relating the child's work to that done by other members of the class, but in large part by analogies to previous work and also with a comparison of the work with the goals of the individual student. Learning the rules of writing is a prolonged process which must be learned as the student recognizes the need for improvement in a particular area. The old idea of learning the process now because it will be needed later carries with it no sense of immediacy for the student.

WHEN SHOULD STUDENTS BEGIN TO WRITE?

Most experts in the language arts field agree that writing should begin soon after the child starts to school. The child should have his first experience of seeing his words transcribed long before he has mastered the mechanics of writing. This means, then, that you must act as the recorder. (The overhead projector is ideal for this type of activity.) There is more than one purpose for this activity. Pride and a sense of accomplishment, as well as an understanding of some of the mechanics of writing, can be established at this age. And, this approach can eliminate the fear which often comes to the uninitiated upper grade student when he encounters his first major writing assignment. Approaching the field of writing positively, then, is our goal.

The primary student requires less motivation for writing than the older students. The beginning student is usually quite anxious to tell his own story, and it is often surprisingly more imaginative than that written by the older student. Literature, tangible objects, and actual experience should provide the basis for most of his early attempts. Since the younger student's attention span is brief, stories should be kept brief for the benefit of the rest of the class. Often, more is accomplished if all of the students participate in telling the same story. You might wish to begin the story, and then let them continue as a group. Several methods can be used, but limiting each student to one sentence encourages concise expression and also helps hold the interest of the other members of the class. Each student builds on the idea given by the previous student. This cooperative exercise is an effective device with which to teach listening and consideration.

Removing Inhibitions

In their early writing attempts, especially in the case of older students who have had very little writing experience, students are often inhibited in their writing to the point where they feel unable to write more than two or three sentences in sequence without feeling threatened. Your first task then is to get them to express themselves in one way or another. Here is one way of accomplishing this:

Give each student a lined piece of paper and specify only that both sides of the paper be filled with written words. Explain to the students that the papers will not be graded and that neither you nor anyone else will read their papers. A ten minute limit is then set. Three or four of these sessions often have surprising effects on the students; most important though, they are no longer quite as hesitant to write.

GETTING STARTED

How is a student stimulated for writing? For the very young student, and for the slow student who has not yet learned to think abstractly, most of the motivation must be concrete; that is, it must appeal to the five senses. For the older and more advanced student, concrete motivation plays an important role too. However, this is a crutch which you may gradually eliminate as the student gains maturity in writing. There is no particular order in which you should introduce creative and descriptive writing related to the five senses, but that this method has value is obvious to the teacher who is concerned that his students write with meaning.

Taste

Give the student some food product such as a carrot, cracker, or pickle. After the students have eaten the item, suggest that they write a description of the taste. A discussion on "Why I liked or disliked it," or treatment of a similar idea, is in order here. A class list of words should be compiled to help them use more concise descriptive language.

crunchy	palatable
sour	rigid
crisp	sweet
tart	tasteless
brittle	firm
savory	luscious
savorless	insipid
relishing	

Listening

Take advantage of sounds near your school. For instance, if you live near a railroad, leave your classroom for a few minutes and listen to an approaching train. (Students should take their writing materials with them, as it is generally best to record impressions while they are hot.) Suggest that they close their eyes and listen very carefully for every sound—the approach of the whistle, the screeching of the brakes, and the sounds as the train moves out of your sound range. This first-hand experience will add color and meaning to students' writing. Later, their writing might relate to other means of transportation—the roar of a motorcycle, the departure of a transport plane, or the combined clatter of city traffic.

Exercises with onomatopoeia (forming a word whose meaning is implied by the sound) help students develop better audio discrimination. If possible, visit a nearby zoo or animal reserve. Let students write their own interpretations of the animal sounds. Encourage them to compare actual sounds with the stereotyped version of animal sounds. For example, is the sound of a duck really "quack"? Students will have more freedom, however, in interpreting the sounds of animals with which they are not familiar, because they will not have learned someone else's translation of the sound.

Sight

Sight is the sense which you will probably wish to develop most extensively. A visit to a nearby museum, factory, or store is an excellent subject for this assignment. After a brief observation period, return to the classroom to record mental impressions. Because of the wide variety of subjects which students can use in their writing, they have more freedom in this area than in the others related to the senses.

An example of motivational literature for visual interpretation which can be used successfully is the autobiographical sketch by Helen Keller, "Three Days to See." Many poems can also be used for motivation of this type. An example of a short motivational poem is "The Runaway" by Robert Frost.

The advent of inexpensive art reproductions has opened a new field in writing. Careful selection of a large variety of different art prints will provide a bank of writing ideas. If further motivation is necessary, involve students more deeply in the assignment by asking leading or provocative questions. Some questions which might be used to elicit worthwhile responses are:

1. How or what do you feel when you look at the picture?
2. Does the setting create a gloomy or a light atmosphere?
3. Does it inspire negative or positive ideas?
4. What ideas are suggested by the picture?
5. What original ideas can you suggest which will add to the interpretation of the picture?

Touch and Smell

Activities similar to the above can be successful in both of these areas. To develop the student's sense of touch, pass objects around the room for students to examine, only by touch. They should be able to determine the texture, size, shape, type of material, weight, etc., just by feeling the object. After they have written their impressions, the object should be passed around the room once more for a comparison of visual and tactile impressions.

A STEP-BY-STEP APPROACH TO WRITING

Observation

Through examination and study of pictures and objects, students can become good observers. That is, they will learn to study pictures, objects, people, and in fact everything in their surroundings, for all details. As they begin to write they will realize that such close scrutiny is of paramount importance and that their writing success depends on it.

Drawing Words

An interesting exercise to teach the intrinsic meanings of words is to have students draw words. For instance, "tall" would be drawn with long vertical letters. "Stocky" would be drawn with short, heavily blocked letters. "Money" might be colored green, "nervous" might be drawn with shaky letters. But, students must first know the meanings of words used, then they can use their imaginations and proceed with the assignment. This exercise can easily be developed into a modified form of the older story-picture method in which actual pictures were substituted for words. An entire paragraph is written with as many words as possible drawn to indicate their meanings. This exercise points up vividly those words whose purpose in a sentence is mainly mechanical. For instance, can you think of a different way to write "a," "the," "of," and "or"?

Choosing the Right Word

To illustrate the importance of using many different words, read a list of common words such as these:

book
box
tree
table
house

Students write a single word to describe each word. After they have completed their list, compare the answers of the same class. In many cases, at least half of the class will have produced the same overused words such as "tall" tree, "big" house, "little" box, etc. Repeat the assignment and again compare answers. Are students using more imagination? You may wish to repeat the assignment using the same words several times.

What's in a Paragraph?

Have each student choose an interesting paragraph of average length for individual analysis. He then lists each separate word he finds in the paragraph and the number of times it appeared. This exercise helps make students aware of the extent to which we use many of our words such as "a," "the," "and," and "an." Through this exercise, they note the words which are used only once. They will soon realize that it is these words which carry most of the ideas which appear in a paragraph.

Personalized Writing

A logical introduction to this segment of the writing program is the "part of a sentence" concerning themselves which is to be completed by the students. For example:

1. My favorite age is_____because . . . .
2. If I had_____I would . . . .
3. When I see_____I think of . . . .
4. Without_____we would . . . .

Initially, expect trite, unimaginative responses such as "without food, we would starve." From average and above average students, though, much more can be expected. In an effort to improve their writing, ask the class to repeat the assignment at least once more, and in some cases three or four times, each time responding differently.

The Autobiography

In most cases, don't ask students to write an autobiography. If you do, don't be chagrined if some disillusioned student opens his drab remarks with "I am eleven years old and I have spent the last five years writing autobiographies." However, you can attain the same results for which this assignment was originally intended by a different approach. Ask them to:

1. Write an objective visual description of themselves. You might ask them to stand before a full-length mirror as they write their detailed description.
2. Have them write "Myself in twenty-five words or less."

3. Have them write "My who's who entry."
4. Another effective way to handle this assignment is to give each student a file card for their self-description and ask them to limit it to one side. This requires very concise writing.

A logical extension of this assignment is to ask students to write an objective description of a classmate.

Giving the Sentence Color

The student need not have a thorough understanding of a sentence before he writes his first paragraph or a complete knowledge of the paragraph before writing his first story. As he writes, he will learn new techniques and become aware of areas of his writing which he can improve. Then, and only then, improvement will result.

After students have become quite involved in writing praxis (actual practice, not busy-work or theory) and have reached the obvious point in their writing where sentence improvement and brief concise expression are most important, introduce several phrases and let them develop worthwhile sentences from them. The phrase must be colorful, interesting, and exciting to the student. A few examples follow:

1. I watched in terror as. . . .
2. Stealthily, he crept. . . .
3. And, then it happened. . . .
4. He was thunderstruck when. . . .
5. Like a streak of lightning, the ball. . . .

Students should try, with similar phrases, to write colorful, descriptive sentences, not just for the sake of using different words, but to transmit ideas clearly and accurately in a readable form. This activity presented in conjunction with longer writing exercises will help students avoid the misconception that a sentence is a single entity in writing.

The word paragraph often discourages a student before the exercise has actually begun. But, as always, fear results from a lack of understanding. A few examples, ranging from

William Faulkner, the master of the long sentence, to Hemingway, the epitome of brief, concise expression, should convince the students that they can set their own limits and goals in writing.

A LOOK AT TECHNIQUE

Learning to write, of course, involves these major steps:
1. A thorough understanding of the sentence.
2. Development of a well-organized paragraph.
3. The combination of paragraphs.
4. Employing figures of speech and other devices which will enhance their writing.

Figures of Speech

SIMILE:	Compares two dissimilar objects with "as" or "like." Ex.: His face looked like a thunderstorm.
PERSONIFICATION:	This figure of speech likens ideas, animals, or objects to human beings—makes inanimate objects lifelike.
METAPHOR:	This process identifies two unlike objects as one—often substitutes one for the other. It is similar to the simile, but it omits the qualifying words, as and like. Ex.: A face of iron, A mushroom of smoke
METONOMY:	Ex.: The kettle boils; a sharp eye; an open ear; to read Shakespeare
HYPERBOLE:	Deliberate overstatement. Ex.: I slipped a mile; I'm dying of curiosity.

PARADOX: This figure of speech contra-
                    dicts, while containing an ele-
                    ment of truth. Ex.: While a great
                    leader may die, he is never ill.
ONOMATOPOEIA: The use of words whose sounds
                    suggest the actual meaning of
                    the word.

Attention-Getting Sentences

Study examples to develop good writing technique. Introduce numerous first sentences from short stories, novels,
news stories, and magazine articles. The sentences should
first of all stimulate the reader's interest. This can be accomp-
plished through a variety of techniques. As each technique
is introduced, students can benefit from a discriminating
search for the particular type of sentence under study. Displays can be made and booklets constructed to give the
assignment more immediate value. The activities to this
point will finally culminate in individual construction of
each type of sentence.

One of these techniques is the creation of interest
through use of an initial phrase which makes a reference to
the past. Some examples are:

One winter years ago. . . .
During the 1920's. . . .
Several generations ago. . . .
At one time in our history. . . .

In a recent class experiment, a class compiled the following group of sentences of the above type:

The story is told that. . . .
It was a time when. . . .
Some years back. . . .
It was in May, 1918. . . .
Just after the first world war. . . .
When Theodore Roosevelt was still president. . . .
On a midsummer day early in the century. . . .

A few years ago. . . .
During the last few years. . . .
The little boy was six years old when. . . .
A lot has happened since. . . .
It's a story they tell. . . .

A DRAMATIC BEGINNING   A dramatic beginning is another favorite technique used by writers. By expanding this technique, even the interest of the most lethargic student can be captured. A few sentences of this type follow:

All during the long night. . . .
I was stopped by those blazing eyes. . . .
The man wounded to the point of death. . . .
Few men are calm when they have only ten minutes
 to live. . . .
I'll forget a lot of things before I forget that
 night. . . .
A large Chicago delivery truck parted the traffic as
 it roared. . . .

SENTENCES WHICH DESIGNATE LOCATION   Designating a particular location is another important technique used in writing. Here are some examples:

Thirty miles north of. . . .
On the northern coast of. . . .
One night in the Philippines. . . .
I sat in my hotel room. . . .
A few miles west of Paris. . . .
In California where the sky seems to be the
 limit. . . .
Snow-capped Mt. Everest. . . .

VARYING THE LENGTH OF SENTENCES   It is important to vary the length of sentences in one's writing. The very short sentence can and usually does catch the eye of the reader. For example:

It was early morning.
The road bent.

It started one Saturday.
He stopped.
"Wait!" he said.

There are many other ways to begin a sentence, but those included are most applicable to elementary students. Regardless of the technique used, the purposes are static:

1. To catch the reader's attention by
   a. Appealing to his imagination.
   b. Drawing on one of his past experiences.
   c. Arousing his curiosity.
   d. Asking a provoking question.
2. To lead him unobtrusively into the story.
3. To put the reader at ease. Even if the material is difficult, the skillful writer conveys the insinuation that it is really not too difficult.
4. To introduce the theme of the material. Although this is not one of the favorite techniques used by writers, it can be effective if not overused.

THE LAST SENTENCE   From this point, let's advance to the last sentence. It is often assigned the difficult task of presenting the last broad generalization of the story or article. In the case of many fiction stories, its assigned duty is to give impact to the story or to climax the story. A few examples of last sentences are:

They called him the sailor.
We heard the rain all night.
When dawn came, nothing was the same.
When I left him, he was still staring at the silver watch.
"We will build it again," he said.
"There will be plenty of other days for climbing," he said.
"Yes," she said, but we knew she was still afraid.
"No," he said, "I sold my coat too."

Another important skill which the writer must master is that of making a smoth transition from paragraph to paragraph. Before practice begins in this area, several models should be studied. Another step is putting a paragraph together. Students should try to avoid long rambling sentences. On the other hand, elimination of the extremely short paragraph is also necessary. A good paragraph for the beginner contains three to eight concise, meaningful sentences. Writing paragraphs can begin in the third and fourth grades. By fifth and sixth grades, students should be able to write two or three consecutive paragraphs.

Learning to Write Conversation

Compare these two paragraphs:

I. "Where have you been?" he asked.

"At the store," she said.

"You were not at the store," he said, "you turned me in. I saw you talking to the policeman."

II. "Where have you been?" he demanded sharply.

"At . . . at the store," she stammered apologetically.

"You were not at the store!" he thundered, growing livid with rage. "You turned me in. I saw you talking to that policeman."

Note the difference between the two sets of conversation. Most of the words are identical. The primary difference lies in the style of the writing. Students' writing can be improved remarkably through concentration on a few basic techniques regarding the writing of conversation.

The first step toward improvement is finding and writing phrases to introduce the speakers in conversation. Overuse of the phrase "he said" greatly detracts from the effectiveness of written conversation. A few substitutes for "he said" are:

He replied	Admitted Mary
He went on to say	Recalled Joe
He continued	He added

He explained	He proceeded
He agreed	She said at last
He reflected	He stammered
He drawled	She said slyly
He announced	She broke in
He snapped	He began
He remarked	Murmured John
Conceded John	She said dryly
Growled James	He replied self-consciously
Answered Elson	

Students should be responsible for compiling their own lists of phrases to improve the writing of conversations.

The second step toward improved written conversation is that of finding acceptable substitutes for "he asked." The same procedure should be followed when working with this phrase. For substitutes, the following may be used:

She inquired anxiously	She begged
She demanded	He wondered
Queried Max	He questioned
He appealed sharply	He challenged

From this point students should be encouraged to incorporate as many of these phrases as possible into their writing. One of the secrets of good writing is variation. Use of inverted order—John said, Said John—is extremely important. Sentence division—"We felt guilty," he said, "but there was nothing we could do"—is also an important means of varying the structure of conversation. Study the following three examples of conversation. All three types should be used in exercises involving conversation:

He said, "If you shout, they will hear us."

"If you shout, they will hear us," he said.

"If you shout," he said, "they will hear us."

Use pictures to develop enthusiasm for writing conversation. Find pictures which show two or more people involved in an animated conversation or discussion. After a careful study of the picture, students may be assigned the task of writing the probable conversation of the individuals shown in the picture. Early experiences in writing conversation should conform to the following format:

MR. X.:

MR. Y:

This style provides greater freedom of expression and less concentration on style. Later, conversation should be written in the conventional manner.

POLISHED WRITING

Eliminating Trite Expressions

Because of their lack of experience in writing, or because of carelessness or some other reason, students tend to overuse many phrases in their writing. In many cases, students will begin to eliminate these as soon as they recognize their offense. Some of the expressions which are to be avoided in writing are:

a far cry
as old as the hills
as black as pitch
by leaps and bounds
twisted my arm
time flew by
easier said than done
far and wide
as good as gold
few and far between
self-made man
howling wind
only time will tell
last but not least
straight as an arrow
a needle in a haystack

cold as ice
hot as a stove
burned his bridges
smart as a whip
sea of faces
greased lightning
light as a feather
wise as an owl
try as he would
too good to be true

Drawing Conclusions

Students can improve their writing if the teacher makes evaluations, learning experiences. Exercises such as the following can teach students to think logically and to draw valuable conclusions. In using such exercises, ask students to give as logical a conclusion for each sentence part as possible:

1. Since radiant energy from the sun does not strike all parts of the earth at the same angle. . . .
2. Since land cools off much more rapidly than water. . . .
3. Since atmospheric conditions a thousand miles away help determine the weather in your hometown. . . .

How Valuable Are Generalities?

The English language contains many general terms. Students tend to misuse these—mainly because they misunderstand their meanings or because they overestimate their effectiveness. To illustrate this to students, ask them to give a specific for each general term below. By noting the wide range of answers, they will realize their ineffectiveness. For instance, a comfortable living for one individual may be quite different from that of a colleague. Similarly, a crowd of people may not have the same meaning in different situations.

Study the generalities in these sentences:

1. Mr. Hudson is an ELDERLY man. (How old is he?)
2. Miss Lincoln was robbed of a SUBSTANTIAL amount of money. (Of how much money was she robbed?)
3. A CONSIDERABLE amount of rain falls in this area annually. (What is the yearly rainfall?)
4. The science class went on OCCASIONAL field trips during the year. (How often did they go?)
5. A CROWD gathered to watch the procession. (How many observers were there?)
6. SEVERAL years ago I lived in San Francisco. (When did I live there?)
7. LARGE QUANTITIES of processed steel left the foundry each day. (How many tons were shipped each day?)

Other general terms are:

many	expensive
often	cheap
seldom	frequently
recently	numerous
meager	regularly

CHECK LIST

1. Are students using a broad list of topics as the basis for their writing?
2. Is student writing being evaluated on an individual basis?
3. Are students inhibited in their writing by past taboos, lists of rules, etc.?
4. Are the initial stages of the writing program

centered around basic elements such as the senses, etc.?

5. Are students drawing material for their writing from observation?

6. Does the writing program allow for the creative use of words as "drawing words"?

7. How adept are students with the major mechanics of writing, such as choosing appropriate titles, paragraphing, good beginning sentences?

8. Do the writing assignments relate to the students?

9. Are students familiar with such techniques as the use of figures of speech to add color to their writing?

10. Are students versatile writers? Can they write convincing dialogue, dialect, free verse, etc.?

11. Do students try to polish their writing by eliminating trite expressions?

12. Are students incorporating their own ideas and opinions into their writing?

8

Developing Writing Skills

Why Write?

Why do you teach writing? Is your list of reasons in agreement with the ones presented here?

1. There is immediate value in writing. Our educational system demands that students be able to express their ideas clearly in writing.
2. We use our writing skills constantly in correspondence, in personal records, in transacting business affairs, in social matters, and even in taking telephone messages.
3. Everything written reflects the skill of the writer. Careless writing often causes misunderstanding.
4. It is a form of expression for which there is no substitute. Writing down ideas is a means of learning to think more logically and a means to clearer expression.

This chapter consists of pertinent writing assignments accompanied by appropriate explanations designed to improve students' writing. Each of these assignments relies heavily on language arts skills already learned.

Writing with Pictures

MATERIALS: Art prints, old magazines, newspapers

One of the most effective writing assignments in the elementary grades is one associated with pictures: art prints, magazine pictures, photographs, etc. The pictures serve as a crutch to the beginning writer whose experiences are very limited and in most cases not developed to the point at which detailed pictures of a scene or event can be formed in the mind and then described adequately on paper. Tangible pictures are used to compensate for this inability in the beginning writer. The pictures can teach him much and help him build a solid groundwork for later writing.

Writing Titles for Pictures

Since a title for a story, article, or picture conveys a great deal of meaning, it is of maximum importance. In many cases, the title determines whether or not the reader will read the story. This initial exercise requires students to be concise, exacting writers, as the title will consist of a very short phrase and in some cases a single word. In the case of many pictures, the title should express the mood. For instance, is the tone of the picture depressing, light-hearted, promising, or threatening? Insist that the titles be specific. Words like happy and sad are too general to be effective except perhaps in the lower grades.

Practice is necessary for the choice of precise words. One type of practice in the case of choosing expressive words to designate a mood is to flash several pictures on a screen, with a slide projector, in rapid succession, and ask students to record their impression of the mood of each. They must think fast, clearly, and accurately if they are to be successful here.

Writing Descriptive Sentences for Pictures

After students have mastered the first step, titling their pictures, they are ready for the next step—writing a one-sentence description of the pictures. Here again, the wording must be precise, as it is to convey the main idea of the picture. In many cases the picture may only suggest an idea, which means that students must use their imaginations to express a worthwhile idea.

After students have completed this assignment, they may wish to prepare an individual or a class booklet of their work.

Writing in Sequence

For this part of the assignment, students find three to five magazine pictures which follow one particular theme or idea, and seem to suggest a story. These pictures should be taken from separate sections of a magazine or from different magazines to avoid using original ideas which have already been written. After finding the pictures, they place them in what they consider to be the best possible sequence. From this point, they proceed to write their story. You may wish to specify that they write only one paragraph to accompany each picture, or they may write a full-length story under the pictures. The title may be written either before or after the story.

THE CHARACTER SKETCH

Perception of human traits has particular significance in the language arts. Determining why one character differs from another is an important part of one's education. This perceptive process will continue throughout the student's life. But, literature is very valuable in broadening students' knowledge of the world outside their own environment. It can also be invaluable to the student in interpreting his own environment. A student may subconsciously partially understand the intangible traits of character possessed by an individual, but confrontation with the characters through study, organization, and recording of thoughts can be a very rewarding experience for the child. To give him some idea of where to begin, you might, with your class, develop criteria for the exercise. The following can be used as a guide:

1. What were your first impressions of the character?
2. Were they correct?
3. What was the single trait which distinguished him from other characters in the story?
4. Can you compare him to anyone you know personally or have met through literature?
5. Is he a *real* character? That is, is he lifelike?
6. Which of his traits brought him success or failure?
7. Is he strong or weak? (In character?)
8. If you could change the main character, what alterations would you make?

Here again, you might use the reverse approach. Establish a list of character traits which might fit one character, then through imaginative writing, *create* the character. Or, as an introductory assignment, students might compile lists of character traits to fit a particular title such as mayor, president, priest, banker, etc. A sample list of traits follows:

1. keen perception
2. shrewd judgment
3. discretion
4. refined sensibility
5. sagacity
6. determination
7. benevolence
8. cautiousness

THE UNFINISHED STORY

The unfinished story is an exercise which you can use in helping students to develop good paragraphs. Distribute copies (or use some visual area in the room) or present the first part of a story orally. It might be the beginning paragraphs of a story which one of your students has written, or the beginning of a short story by a well-known author. Let students finish the story in their own way. Later, you might like to make this type of exercise a cooperative effort—building the story sentence by sentence. This process will require carefully organized thought. Each student must build on the previous sentence. To prevent discouragement and wordy writing, never set a specific length for this type of writing.

The story beginning which you use should be short and exciting. The story beginning itself should be interesting enough to provide motivation for further writing on the story. Here is a sample:

> I was jarred out of a sound sleep. I stared at the luminescent radium hands of the clock on the bedside stand. The time was 2:21 A.M. I heard the noise again. Something was being dragged into the room across the hall. I heard more shuffling at the bottom of the stairs. I crawled out of bed as quietly as possible. . . .

Sometimes when presenting the story beginning, the unfolding technique is best. That is, write the story beginning on adding machine tape and pull it through an opaque projector; the students read it as you do so.

A Group Project

After dividing the class into small groups, distribute an interesting beginning sentence to each group. Each student in the group writes one sentence of the story. The story is circulated through the group until it is completed. Together, the group titles the story and proofreads it.

WRITING IN SOCIAL STUDIES

Incorporate writing into as many phases of the curriculum as possible. Social studies are conducive to writing with meaning. A typical assignment will best demonstrate the effectiveness of writing in social studies. Again, keeping to the premise that students should choose their own topics, give them a general topic, usually one related to the unit being studied, then let them think of their own specific topic.

A typical situation is the study of the Soviet Union. Someone might suggest that the class write reports. Then, as a class, discuss possible subject areas. A list of suggestions for writing follows:

1. I was a secret agent in the U.S.S.R.
2. A visit to the Kremlin.
3. The "making" of a collective farm.
4. My job as a newspaper reporter.
5. A day in a Soviet school.

The Field Trip

The field trip can be very effective in learning. Even the field trip, however, must be planned with imagination. Preparation for the trip should involve some writing such as a letter requesting permission to visit the particular place chosen by the class. Also, an exercise discussing what they hope to gain from the field trip is in order. The broadened aspect of the social studies will permit a very wide range of choice for your trip. You might visit a bank while studying about economics; an Indian reservation, a ghetto, a suburb, or the Chinese section of your city while studying social conditions; city hall while studying government; the library, post office, and other public buildings while discussing the community; or you might wish to do original research of a particular area on your tour. One recent experience which came to my attention was a close search for Indian artifacts in an old Indian village. Another involved watching a group of archaeologists at work in an excavation area. Still another was an excursion through a building under construction. All of these experiences provided a rich background for writing when the student was back in the classroom.

WRITING A REPORT

I. CHOOSE THE TITLE

Choosing the subject is a very important skill. Limiting it so that it can be fitted into the boundaries of a report, though, is often difficult for the elementary student. Though difficult at first, the choice of a topic should be designated to the student.

II. OUTLINING

The material for the report should be outlined. If more than four topics are used in the outline, the topic is probably too broad, and it should be limited.

III. BEGINNING AND ENDING SENTENCES

The purpose of writing the beginning and ending sentences before beginning the actual writing of the report is to set the limits of the report. The beginning sentence establishes the theme and indicates the scope of the topic. The concluding sentence reasserts the theme and makes some reference as to the thoroughness of the report.

IV. BEGINNING AND ENDING PARAGRAPHS

It is often helpful, in addition to writing the beginning and ending sentences, to write the beginning and ending paragraphs at this point. These two steps will usually be combined.

V. THE MIDDLE PARAGRAPHS

The final step of the actual writing is the completion of the middle paragraphs. These paragraphs will contain most of the facts and ideas of the report. These paragraphs, as well as all parts of the report, should be carefully written.

VI. PROOFREADING

Proofreading material twice is a good habit for students to form.

THE NEWSPAPER

The following is an outline of a unit on the newspaper. One of the purposes for including it here is to show the importance of writing in any unit.

MATERIALS

Sample newspapers (enough for each student for two or more days)
Magazines

PURPOSES

To teach the format of a newspaper.
To stimulate interest in current affairs.
Through advertising—teach critical analysis of printed material.

Give students an opportunity to create their own advertisements using original ideas in writing and in artistic design.

PROCEDURE

    I. What is the dateline of a news story?
    II. What are newspaper headlines?
    III. What is a lead paragraph?
    IV. What information can be found in the lead paragraph?
    V. What kind of information is found on the front page?
    VI. What is meant by a news scoop?
    VII. Where is the index?
    VIII. What is the editorial page?
    IX. Find one of the regular columns. Who are these columns written for?
    X. Where are the television and radio listings?
    XI. What is contained on the social page?
    XII. What other special sections can you find?
    XIII. What part of the paper do you like best (excluding comics)? Why?

GROUP WORK

Divide into groups of three or more.

Group I: Find and report on the main state news story.

Group II: Find and report on the main national news story.

Group III: Find and report on the main international news story.

Group IV: Find and report on one science news article.

Group V: Find and report on one or two sports articles.

Group VI: Have one group report on miscellaneous material found in the paper.

Groups VII, VIII, etc.: Other fields such as oceanography, anthropology, etc. may be included in the reports.

BULLETIN BOARD

1. A large international map should be placed at the focal point.
2. An interesting caption, such as "News Flashes," should be used. Encourage students to think of possible captions.
3. Students bring news articles (high interest with impressionable pictures) to place on the bulletin board. Yarn can then be used to indicate the setting of the news article. (An excellent geography-teaching technique.)
4. On each news article, students place captions or explanatory phrases. These comments should show creativity as well as understanding of the article.

FOLLOW-UP

1. In conjunction with this bulletin board, have students listen to a recorded newscast and from the information they receive, write the lead paragraph for a news story.
2. Place these news stories on the board.
3. A class or individual booklet can be made to show a series of important events.

This study of journalism is necessary, and it is logical that it should begin with a study of the news article. Study several articles, noting headings, subheadings, and the arrangement of facts and ideas. Call attention to the first part of the article, which contains the basic facts and ideas; then, to the descriptive part of the article. After students have familiarized themselves with the journalistic style, let them try their hand at writing some sample newspaper articles. Exercises should be arranged in this order:

1. Study sample newspaper and other articles.
2. Report on some classroom or school activity.
3. Conduct interviews, using well-written questions.
   a. First within your classroom
   b. Then with members of other classes
   c. Interviews outside of school
4. Write and actually send editorials to magazines and newspapers.
5. Write letters to the editor and send sample letters.
6. Write a column—this could be posted in the classroom. It should be a classroom project with a staff of three or four volunteers, with the entire class submitting ideas. It might be a problem-solving column, or an ideas column.
7. Write a comic strip. (This activity will provide an opportunity for the artistic members of the class.) This activity should continue for several days until interest wanes.
8. Using large cardboard, make a mock-up of a newspaper front page. Make it as realistic as possible with appropriate headlines, datelines, etc. It should be marked off in columns. This activity is usually most effective if it is done to celebrate some holiday or major event.

After developing interest and skill in all of these activities you are ready to develop your own newspaper. This paper should be as realistic as possible. It can and should involve every area of the curriculum and every member of the class. New ideas in science, current events, the latest art work, a story, poetry, quotations, and other fillers, and the editorial page complete with letters to the editor, the comic page, and news articles should comprise the paper. Pictures to accompany news stories could be taken from old edition newspapers for the display edition. The editorial staff, chosen according to their writing and organizational skills, should be responsible, with your direction, for content and style. The paper, however, should be a cooperative effort of the entire class. Your proofreaders are responsible for correcting the final copy. It is possible that some members of the class can type well enough to produce the stencils. Your last step, then, is the reproduction and distribution of the paper. Hard work and careful planning can produce a paper of which the class can be very proud. This could well be your most important teaching situation in the entire language arts curriculum. (Many newspapers are happy to supply enough papers for the class for individual study if you request them and explain the purpose of the request. They would also be glad to have you visit their printing establishments.) Because of the large amount of work such an activity involves for both students and teacher, you may wish to produce only one or two papers during the year. However, some teachers find that a monthly paper fits their class needs best.

THE COMMERCIAL IN THE CLASSROOM

Concise and imaginative writing results from units patterned after commercial advertising. Commercial advertisers demand a high degree of creative talent which can be converted into a form which appeals to the public, and benefit can be derived from the study of this medium. A first unit on advertising should begin with a well-organized study of advertisements. Pay particular notice to "pet" advertising terms such as NEW, CLEANER, FRESHER, BETTER, MORE, etc. (better than what? cleaner than what?) After skill in this area has been developed, students can begin to develop their own advertisements. The topics for these might be real or imaginary products. Developmental steps should include:

1. Choosing the topic
2. Writing the jingle or slogan
3. Creating an art scheme to go along with your slogan

Your goals should be to appeal to the reader, both by the written words and by the art scheme. Stress the importance of discriminatory writing—that is, giving the reader a true picture of the product being advertised. Steer clear of propaganda techniques. If correctly used, advertising is a means of teaching better writing techniques.

Advertisements Must:

1. Catch the eye of the observer.
2. Make the viewer think of something which will sell him the product. In other words, the advertisements must appeal to the person's background experiences. For example, a soup advertisement is shown in a winter setting and "stops winter cold" is the caption. The viewer may remember that soup seems to taste particularly good on cold days, and he makes a purchase.
3. Suggest that all of your friends either have bought or are planning to purchase the product. "Join . . . ," "YOU'RE . . . ," etc. are examples of these beginnings.
4. Make the reader, listener, or viewer think the product will improve him in some way.

Advertisements Use Slogans and Proverbs

Have students find advertisements which use these techniques. Later they may wish to write their own version of these techniques. Experience with each of these phases of advertising is basic to understanding the commercial.

Popular phrases: Teen-age jargon often is included in advertisements. Slang expressions such as those often used in advertising appeal to elementary students. This is one way of broadening the understanding of language.

Comparisons: Many advertisements use at least one of the degrees of comparison: positive, good; comparative, better; superlative, best. Words like more, most, better, longer, taller, less, etc. are popular words; and in fact, they form the basis for much of our advertising.

Directives: See your . . . , Buy now . . . , Try the . . . , Let us . . . .

Questions: Tired of . . . ? Afraid to . . . ? Are you the only . . . ? The last of . . . ? When was the last . . . ?

Riddles: What is . . . ? How long is . . . ?

Negatives: Advertisements which use such words as *never, don't, no,* etc. fit into this category.

Conditionals: Many of the conditional advertisements begin with *if.*

"How to" advertisements: These advertisements usually begin with the words *How to,* and proceed to explain how something can be done more easily, more cheaply, etc.

Catchy phrases: Many advertisements use catchy phrases. These have a great deal of interest for elementary students. They are part of the advertising appeal.

Suggestions: Maybe it's . . . , Why not . . . ? Do you remember . . . ?

Favorite words in advertising: new, breakthrough, reduced, increased

Alliteration: This device repeats first sounds as a part of the advertising appeal. Sometimes the same word or phrase may be repeated several times in a single advertisement. This repetition fixes the name of the product or the advertising slogan firmly in the prospective buyer's mind.

Testimonials: Famous people speak for these advertisers.

Follow-up

1. Students should now write their advertisements. They should use interesting phrases and artistic design.
2. These can be used very effectively in a bulletin board display. (Letters cut from magazines for the bulletin board can be very attractive.)
3. A classroom billboard can be constructed sometime during the unit. This is a group project. The completed billboard should look, as much as possible, like a highway billboard.

DESIGNING LABELS   Much can be learned from an exercise in design. The first step is to examine the labels on a number of commercial packaged goods: glues, powdered products, liquid products, etc. Students pay particular attention to the instructions for use printed on the label, the ingredients, and any other information they consider pertinent.

An extension of this assignment is to design the entire label in the following steps:

1. Draw the artistic designs.
2. Place the words identifying the product at the focal point, or the most eye-catching position.
3. Print descriptive words which would appeal to the consumer.
4. Transfer instructions for use to the label.
5. Place the trademark, weight, and any other necessary information on the label.

OTHER WRITING ACTIVITIES

1. Write campaign slogans
   a. For political campaigns.

    b. For community projects and campaigns such as youth movements.
2. Write clear, concise directions, telling someone how to operate some type of mechanical device.
3. Write plays which can be used in the classroom.
4. Write the words to go along with music written in music class.
5. Write a story about something which has never existed. (This will give you an opportunity to again incorporate art into language arts—suggest drawings or other art projects which go along with their stories.)
6. Rewrite old stories and poetry from literature, in present-day vernacular. Shakespeare, Chaucer, or Milton can be used for the upper grades. (Use the reverse of this exercise also.)
7. Write newspaper accounts about some historic event such as reports on President Lincoln's assassination, the pony express, and the first successful airplane flight.

CHECK LIST

1. Are you satisfied that your reasons for teaching writing are ideal?
2. Are you using audio-visual aids to improve your writing program?
3. Do the students learn to interpret their own environment through the writing program?
4. Is writing an important part of every subject area?
5. Are you using outside sources and materials to enliven the writing program?
6. How adept are students at locating and compiling information for a report?
7. Are you using a wide variety of material; for ex-

ample, the newspaper, to stimulate interest in writing?

8. Are group work, bulletin boards, projects, and original research part of the writing program?

9

Effective Writing
Assignments

The good writer must be able to express what he sees if he is to write effectively. He must tell enough to let the reader see too, and in the telling, he must create enough interest to lead the reader on, sentence after sentence, into the story, article, or essay. The effective writer must choose the right word.

Especially for the beginning writer, finding the right word means extensive use of the dictionary. As his vocabulary is enlarged, however, more and more often the right word will seem to simply fall into place.

Writing for the beginner, or for the professional, for that matter, is not easy. Writing requires rigid self-discipline and inner as well as exterior motivation.

But writing can be fun too. A sense of satisfaction and pride rewards the writer when some piece of work has been carefully planned and well-polished. This is part of the immediate value. The student soon learns, too, that a great deal of future value can be derived from learning to write.

By the end of the fourth grade, the elementary student should have learned to write interesting sentences. His sentences should be varied in length, as well as in style. By this time he should be able to write simple, complex, and compound sentences with little difficulty. He should also be able to effectively use both inverted sentences and the very short sentence. The real test of his skill, though, is not whether he can simply write the type of sentence specified, but if he can write an interesting, concise, and correct paragraph and whether he can express his ideas well.

By the end of the fourth grade, some students will not have mastered the art of writing good sentences and good paragraphs. Some students will still be struggling with these basic elements of writing at the end of sixth grade or even junior high. Lack of skill in this area *must not* be excused with the fallacious statement that writing is a talent for which some students have an innate talent and others do not. It is true that some students have the ability to write creatively while others seem to lack this, but with average or even near average intelligence, almost any student can learn to write interesting and well-constructed sentences which express worthwhile ideas.

Throughout the fifth and sixth grades the teachers have the task, often a difficult one, of developing the student's skill in the mechanics of writing as well as an interest in and a flair for writing. These tasks can be accomplished through a systematic series of motivating and stimulating writing projects.

OBSERVATION AND DESCRIPTION

"In a sense, students must pass through a descriptive phase before they can be cleared for other more comprehensive writing. To emphasize this idea by an analogy, description is like physical technique to a musician: it is of limited value by itself, but no important ideas are any good without it." [1]

This idea applies to the writer in the intermediate grades.

Example Assignment Number I

Write a descriptive paragraph. The field of possible topics is extremely broad, but don't spend a great deal of time choosing a topic. Almost anything you are familiar with can serve as your first subject But, for this first assignment, choose a simple object for description. Don't use a person or an animal as the subject for this assignment. You may wish to choose one of the following as your topic:

a. A tree outside your classroom window. (Remember you are taking the place of the artist. The reader can see only what you put on your paper.)

b. The winding river you crossed on your way to school.

c. The sidewalk which runs in front of your home. (Note irregular cracks, grass growing through it, etc.)

d. A well-read book.

e. The burned-out forest you saw on your vacation.

f. A small midwestern town you once passed through. (Give it a name like Purdum, Dunning, or Thedford.)

STUDENT EXAMPLE I

"The old house stood on a hill near the town. The wood was rotted near the ground. Most of the plaster had fallen from the walls. The windows had been broken out and the wind whistled through it. The once beautiful stairway had

---

[1] Hart Day Leavitt and David A. Sohn, *Stop, Look, and Write!* (N.Y.: Bantam Books), 1964, p. 222.

now only a few steps left in it. Upstairs, an old doll with the arms gone lay near a cot. It was a very sad place."

STUDENT EXAMPLE II

"The damp white fog smelled as fresh as a soft April shower. Light from the dripping orange and black school bus reflected on the dense fog. The light could not penetrate it. The windows were as steamy as a bathroom mirror after a hot bath."

STUDENT EXAMPLE III

"The noisy train came roaring through the small town of Halsey. The horn tooted a couple of times and then it was gone. It was on its way to another small town west of here."

Learning to Write by Example

Even elementary students can learn to write by studying examples of good description by well-known authors. Examples such as the following are interesting as a source for study and comparison.

EXAMPLE I (*To Kill a Mockingbird*, Harper Lee)

"Maycomb was an old town, but it was a tired old town when I first knew it. In rainy weather the streets turned to red slop; grass grew on the sidewalks, the courthouse sagged in the square."

EXAMPLE II (*Travels with Charley*, John Steinbeck)

"Some American cities are like badger holes, ringed with trash—all of them—surrounded by piles of wrecked and rusting automobiles, and almost smothered with rubbish."

OBSERVATION

Observation is really the most accessible and most effective key to good writing. Is the student really seeing? Is he really observing? Is he writing the details which will interest the reader and make his piece of writing believable?

That a branch is broken far up in a tree or that the bottom step of the old house is crumbling, or that there is the imprint of a foot in the sidewalk are descriptive points which may add to a story.

In almost all cases of good writing, the writer has worked very hard to use all of the right words and to get every word in just the right place. Such perfection often requires many rewrites. Good writing doesn't just happen. In *A Moveable Feast*, Ernest Hemingway said of his early years of writing, "It often took me a full morning of work to write a single paragraph."

Too much required rewriting and tedious reworking of a paragraph discourages many elementary students. Therefore, it should be suggested, but not made compulsory. It is very often advisable to evaluate a student's writing on the basis of its creativeness, uniqueness, and interest. The student must, however, accept the fact that readability is important—the mechanics, appearance of the paper, etc. Occasionally it may be helpful to suggest that an article be rewritten if the need for improvement is extremely obvious. Students, too, need to recognize the importance of a single word. Changing one word can often improve a paragraph significantly.

Three important rules to remember when writing:
   a. Begin your sentences in various ways. Too many sentences which begin with *the, he,* and *it,* for instance, may make the reader lose interest.
   b. Change the pattern for your sentences. Invert sentences occasionally. Use simple, complex, and compound sentences when writing.

c. Vary the length of your sentences. Very short sentences help to attract attention, and they also break the monotony in a piece of writing.

Assignment II

To give you more practice in writing description, describe an animal. Remember what you have learned so far about clear, concise writing. Here is a good example of animal description from *Cannery Row*, by John Steinbeck.

"A well-grown gopher took up residence in a thicket of mallow weeds in the vacant lot on Cannery Row. It was a perfect place. The deep green luscious mallows towered up crisp and rich and as they matured their little cheeses hung down provocatively. The earth was perfect for a gopher hole too, black and soft and yet with a little clay in it so that it didn't crumble and the tunnels didn't cave in. The gopher was fat and sleek and he had always plenty of food in his cheek pouches. His little ears were clean and well set and his eyes were as black as old fashioned pin heads and just about the same size. His digging hands were strong and the fur on his back was glossy brown and the fawn-colored fur on his chest was incredibly soft and rich. He had long curving yellow teeth and a little short tail. Altogether he was a beautiful gopher and in the prime of his life."

(Try to make this description somewhat longer than the first you did.)

Assignment III

Write a description of a person. This first description of a person should be of someone other than yourself. Again, follow the rules already established, and be as objective as possible in reporting how you see the person. Remember that often the simplest sentences are the most readable and therefore the most effective.

EXAMPLE A ("Death in the Woods," Sherwood Anderson)

"She was an old woman and lived on a farm near the town in which I lived."

EXAMPLE B ("A Clean, Well-Lighted Place," Ernest Hemingway)

"It was late and everyone had left the cafe except an old man who sat in the shadow the leaves of the tree made against the electric light."

Assignment IV

Write a description of yourself. This description should not involve character traits, but only observable points. Sit in front of a mirror and study your image very carefully. Record what you see.

Assignment V

Observe and write a description of something in motion. Possible topics are:
   a. A cat trying to capture a bird.
   b. A dog that is chasing a cat.
   c. A horse marching proudly in a parade.
   d. A train in motion (Describe it in detail—as it approaches, as it sways when turning a curve, and then becomes smaller in the distance).

EXAMPLE A ("The Horse Dealer's Daughter," D. H. Lawrence)

"The great draught-horse swung past."

EXAMPLE B ("The White Quail," John Steinbeck)

"The white quail dipped her beak again and threw back her head to swallow."

Descriptive writing often makes use of figures of speech. Metaphors and similes are favorite devices writers use to add color to their writing.

EXAMPLE A *(Travels with Charley,* John Steinbeck)

"The customers were folded over their coffee cups like ferns."

EXAMPLE B *(Kon-Tiki,* Thor Heyerdahl)

"The jungle stood LIKE A SOLID WALL along the banks on both sides, and parrots and other bright-colored birds fluttered out of the dense foliage as we passed. Once or twice, an alligator hurled itself into the river and became invisible in the muddy water."

Descriptive writing plays a part in almost every type of writing the student will do. Even when writing letters, the letter becomes more readable, and thus more effective, when description is used. The goal students should work toward is: No word is misplaced, there are no extra words, and the piece of writing conveys the exact meaning the writer intended.

CREATIVE WRITING

Creative writing is the stuff fiction is made of. John Steinbeck, Ernest Hemingway, William Faulkner, and Pearl Buck are among the modern authors whom we consider masters of the art of creative writing. But for all of them, learning to write well was a difficult process. Your students may never be Hemingways or Steinbecks, but they can learn to write creative material that will hold the interest of other readers and provide another outlet of expression for them.

Assignment I

Observe some person (any age) you do not know and write a short fictional account of some part of his life. You may choose to write about someone you observed at some other time, who impressed you and whom you remember very distinctly. The following examples of topics should indicate to you the type of subject you might use for this assignment:

    a. An elderly woman you saw waiting nervously on a park bench.
    b. A lonely man in an art gallery.
    c. A twelve year old boy deep in thought ambling slowly down the street.
    d. The down-and-out man you saw the policemen arrest.
    e. The middle-aged woman you see every morning on her way to work.

Remember what you have learned to this point about descriptive writing. Use description, but tell a story at the same time.

EXAMPLE A (*When the Legends Die,* Hal Borland)

"Winter passed. New leaves came again to the aspens, then to the oaks, and the surging streams quieted and spring was upon them. They fished. They picked serviceberries, then chokecherries. They made meat and dried it. And the boy was big enough to help with all these things. Then the leaves fell and ice came, and snow whitened Pagosa Peak once more. Another winter passed, with its wailing storms, its roaring snow-slides, its shrunken days. And no one came, neither Blue Elk nor the sheriff nor anyone looking for them."

EXAMPLE B ("The Sculptor's Funeral," Willa Cather)

"A group of the townspeople stood on the station siding of a little Kansas town, awaiting the coming of the night train, which was already twenty minutes overdue."

Assignment II

Write a tall-tale, science fiction type of story. You may decide to make yourself one of the main characters in this story. The purpose of this assignment is to break away from the well-established lines of writing and write something which is your own creation—something which has never been written before.

Assignment III

Write your first story. Don't try to be overly dramatic, though. Beginning writers often agonize at length over a lack of topics for stories. The fact is that there is an abundance of material, but the writer must choose a topic which fits his style and gives it life. Many good stories have been written about rather insignificant topics.

"Big Two-Hearted River" by Ernest Hemingway, for instance, is by no means a dramatic story. Nick, the character in the story, goes on foot to a sparsely populated area to fish and to recover from an injury. There is no major plot— no particularly high or low point in the story.

Similarly, "The Enchanted Bluff" by Willa Cather is not a story of high excitement, but it is a story about people and a myth they created; and thus it has interest for many readers.

Assignment IV

Write a story about one incident which happened to you or to which you were an observer or were closely related. Again don't spend a great deal of time searching for the unusual. Try, however, to make your article unique and in your own style.

Assignment V

Write a creative story based on newspaper headlines. Choose interesting and unique topics. *Examples:*
   a. Strange Object Sighted
   b. Disappearance; Still Mystery
   c. Money Found

10

Building Reading Skills

A variety of factors motivate children to read. The strongest motivating force, but not necessarily the most effective one, is the school's compulsory requirements. The most effective motivation is self-directed. That is, the prospective reader must have an inner compulsion to read. He realizes the importance of reading and proceeds as well as he can to build the necessary reading skills independently. Educators are the first to admit that the first approach is a poor one.

A third type of motivation is a search for enjoyment through reading. A teacher's own enthusiasm for reading stimulates children to read for enjoyment. A teacher in the lower grades encourages reading by telling stories to the class. If the teacher has chosen stories that interest the children, they will soon be searching out books on their own for reading. Films, tapes, and records based on stories and books also encourage students to read.

Finally, the search for knowledge is the most important reason for reading, even though elementary students may not yet realize this fact. Preschool children evidence this desire with the frequent repetition of "What does it say?" The intensity of this desire greatly increases and influences the amount and quality of the material which a student reads.

The avid reader is very often the one who succeeds as a student, as a career person, etc. He succeeds because he has gained insight into people's lives and into their actions, and because he has experienced so much of life vicariously that he has time left for living his life with clear direction. He succeeds because he has a broad resource of knowledge, gleaned from books.

Reading Skills: Speed, Vocabulary, Concentration, Oral Reading

A student's reading speed will depend to a great extent on the type of material being read, on his ability, and on his motivation. Poetry will not be read at the same rapid pace used to read a newspaper. History, short stories, novels, and even directions require singular reading speeds. Reading speed is an individual matter. In a classroom of thirty students, it is not unlikely that thirty different time intervals will be recorded during the reading of a single selection.

Teachers often ask, "How can reading speed be increased without sacrificing comprehension and without pressuring the child unduly?" Many have said, "The answer is simple." I would like to make a qualified counter statement. It is *not* easy, but it is a goal which can be reached by the ambitious, conscientious student. In the first place, the most effective method of increasing speed and at the same time improving comprehension is to *read*. At first glance this may seem ambiguous, nevertheless, practice in reading material of interest and of an acceptable ability level is the key to higher speed and increased comprehension. Practice in reading all types of materials to gain reading versatility is the good reader's responsibility and as he practices, even though he may give very little attention to his reading speed, his reading pace will increase. There are various techniques which can be used to increase reading speed, and for the student who is particularly slow, these may be employed.

SCANNING   Very often it is not necessary to let the eyes rest on every word. The eyes can be trained to note only important words as they move rapidly down the page. This we call scanning. It is a technique often used in reading a newspaper, or a particularly light or easy story. Its value lies in the fact that while not sacrificing comprehension (to the skillful scanner) more can be read in much less time. This, like all types of reading, however, requires much practice.

A very simple but effective means of increasing reading speed is that of moving a file card as rapidly as possible down the page. This technique prevents the reader from retracing what he has read, thus stressing the importance of comprehension during the first reading. Each time a student reads he should move the card a little more rapidly in a conscious effort to improve speed. This technique, however, should not become an indispensable crutch. It should be used for only a short period of time, and then the reader should read for a time without it, without lapsing back into poor reading habits.

Very often the major difficulty of slow readers is that they are silently forming each word with their tongue and other speech organs. Quite often slow readers are not even aware of this habit. One simple correctional method frequently used is that of holding a small file card between the teeth for a short period of time. This makes students aware of the movement of the lips and tongue, and after this awareness they can consciously begin to speed up the eye to brain transfer by avoiding the oral speech parts.

READING AND VOCABULARY   One of the advantages of reading is an enlarged vocabulary. As a student reads, it is inevitable that his vocabularies—oral, reading, and written —will increase. The teacher should, however, encourage the reading of all types of materials: children's novels, short stories, newspapers, children's magazines, etc. in an effort to improve vocabulary.

INDEPENDENT READING   Many students seldom read independently because they find reading tedious. They lack the self-discipline which reading requires. Here, the teacher can help the child by giving him interesting materials to read. Too, encourage him to read completely short stories and articles. Eventually, the child will learn to read and appreciate full-length books.

Reading Comprehension

CHECKING MAIN EVENTS   We read mainly for ideas. For this reason, main ideas are necessarily stressed most. After reading a story, the main question is, "What is the single most important idea of the story?" This is logically followed by a discussion of the other principal ideas couched in the story. Questions leading to the discovery of main ideas may take a form similar to the following:

Students frequently have difficulty singling out main ideas in a story. For this reason, it is best to first present a choice. For instance, "Is the main idea of the story A, B, or C?" Later, after numerous experiences with this type of practice, students will be better able to give the main idea independently. Then you may simply ask them, "What is the main idea in this story?" After the principal theme of the story has been established, related questions can greatly enhance the understanding of the story. Here is a list of questions which can be used with most stories:

1. Would you have reacted the same way if you had been the main character?
2. What is the setting of the story?
3. Was this the best setting for this type of story?
4. Why do you think the author chose_____ as his theme?
5. Did the author ever visit the actual setting for the story?
6. Choose another possible title for the story.

7. Which sentence do you believe to be the most important one in the story?
8. For whom was the story written?
9. Give examples of figures of speech used.
10. Write a sequel to the story.

CHECKING FOR DETAILS   Check for important details. Details are important if other ideas depend on them. For instance, knowing that the main character was wearing a blue coat can be considered an important detail only if ensuing events depend on that fact. In reading detective stories, students should be particularly conscious of physical details.

Here is an exercise which is helpful in teaching students to place events in chronological order. The same procedure may be used for much of the literature used in elementary school. In each of the following sentences, two events are mentioned. Circle the event that occurred first. If the events occurred simultaneously, leave the sentence as it is:

1. As the firemen helplessly watched, the building burned to the ground.
2. Before he had finished his explanation, the irate customer left the store.
3. The plane had been in the air for only a few minutes when mechanical difficulties developed.
4. While waiting for his friend, he read the evening paper.
5. It was dark when they left the playground.

FACT OR OPINION?   Understanding the difference between facts and ideas is crucial to critical reading. Many commonly used phrases introduce opinions and theories. Here are a few:

are believed to have been
are thought to be
probably the most important

has been considered
may indicate
it is likely that
it is generally agreed that
suggests that
Facts are presented in a more authoritative manner. The following is an exercise in critical reading. Students should study facts and opinions similar to the following and determine which are facts and which are theories or opinions.

a. World War II ended in 1945.
b. The strange animal apparently became extinct several thousand years ago.
c. The production of steel in the United States increased last year.
d. He is credited with having made the most important scientific contribution of the century.
e. No record exists of any human life in that area.
f. Interplanetary travel may be possible in the future.

LISTING EVENTS   Listing events chronologically is important in the development of a literary selection. When listing events, however, list them according to their actual happening. In other words, pay particular attention to flashbacks (those parts of the story which refer the reader to an earlier time and setting). Quite often events in a story will not be listed in the exact order in which they occurred. The story may begin at one time, relate back a decade or more, then end in the same period of time in which the story was begun. Listing main events may be an individual project, a group assignment, or the responsibility of the whole class. This assignment, too, may be either written or oral.

QUOTATIONS   An important method of checking student comprehension of literature is the use of quotations. Choose direct quotations from the story. Read these aloud and ask students to name the speaker. Choose these quotations carefully; that is, choose those which are most representative of the main characters in the story. For a written check, list from five to ten quotations for students to identify. Read the quotation only once. This encourages careful listening and thought.

FICTION

A work of literature based on imagination which takes a form which could conceivably be realistic is fiction. The characters are not actual people, but they are either patterned after some person or they are the composite impressions the author has of a particular type of person. The novel, short stories, etc. are classed under this category. Other works of literature can be broadly grouped under nonfiction.

Literature

In its broad sense, literature is everything which has ever been written. Books, newspapers, and magazines all fall into this category. In a narrower sense, relating to the school, literature is written material which has definite educational merit. Material which treats old ideas in a new way is literature. Literature in its finest sense is a synthesis of man's greatest ideas. But to effect this synthesis, a number of factors must be considered.

PROSE   Stories, novels, newspapers, magazines, etc. are written in prosaic form. It is the ordinary form of written or oral language. The opposite form is poetry.

THE NOVEL   The novel is of little concern in the elementary school. Avid readers may acquaint themselves with this art form in the upper intermediate grades and in junior high school, independently, but seldom will major novels have any part in the organized curriculum. Many books of novel length, however, will be presented in elementary school. Recognizing the novel as an art form, being aware of some of the most prominent authors, and perhaps reading or listening to excerpts from novels constitutes the use of the novel, at least in its truest form, in the elementary school.

CLASSICS   A book or story is placed under this category if it has consistently been popular for a period of fifty or more years.

Elements of the Novel

SETTING   When you, the teacher, introduce a story to your students, potential readers, there are a number of technical aspects of the story which you must consider. In the first place, the setting is important. In many instances, understanding the characters is dependent on understanding where the action occurred, and when. This is the setting. For instance, in *Island of the Blue Dolphins* by Scott O'Dell, you might ask how the lonely island setting affected the story.

Students should recognize both the general and the specific settings. For instance, in Pearl Buck's *Big Wave*, the general setting is Japan, but more specifically, the setting is along the coast, and the idea of the story is based on this setting. In reading, it is also necessary to note details of the setting. The climax of the story may depend on a minor detail.

PLOT   The plot encompasses the visible action in the story. It is the totality of events following a pattern. The plot is the plan, the map, the intrigue of the story. The form of the plot depends on the author and on the characters he has created. A commonly used traditional form of plot is a gradually increased tempo of action or feeling leading to a climax or crisis, which fades into a declining pattern of action.

In another type of story the action gradually rises until the story ends with a final climactic impact. Authors use many variations of these two types of plots. Elementary students, while not overly concerned with all of the nuances of authorial plots, can gain a much deeper insight into the meaning of a story by considering them.

THE FLASHBACK   A flashback is the part of a story which refers the reader back to an earlier time. If students know the purpose of a flashback—to relate past happenings in as dramatic a way as possible—they will easily understand the chronology of the story. Sentence beginnings which introduce a flashback may begin in the following ways:

Mrs. Seaton had been. . . .

That was two years after. . . .

Then something else happened. . . .

I remember it was the second week in April. . . .

EPILOG   An epilog is the concluding section added to a work of literature.

CHARACTER   A great deal can be done with the characters in the story. For instance, students can write a character sketch, as mentioned earlier, dramatize the character, etc.

The elementary student should recognize the two main characters in a novel—the antagonist, and the protagonist. The antagonist of a story or book is the leading foe or force which causes hostile action against the hero. The protagonist is the hero of the story.

POINT OF VIEW   The way a story is told adds to or detracts from the effectiveness of the story and is usually referred to as point of view. Three different points of view are commonly used.

I. FIRST PERSON

The first person point of view is exactly what the term states: The author is the key figure in the story and he refers to himself as "I" or "me." In some cases the author takes the form of the key person. From another first person point of view, the author is an obscure character whose main task is simply that of reporting the action. The following two examples illustrate this technique:

A. I laid the book down, crossed the room, and confronted the man.

B. He was afraid of me. He crept slowly forward.

First person is, of course, used in autobiographies. The technique is often used in an attempt to add an air of authenticity.

II. PERSONA

The second technique, the use of a persona, occurs when the author assumes the role of reporter. He reports happenings and records conversations between characters. However, an author who uses this form usually limits his outlook to one character. The entire story is told entirely from the one standpoint. Third person is used. This point of view is often used by the author as a means of introducing more characters into the story and involving them in the core of the story. Examples are:

A. He stood patting the horse, oblivious to everything else.

B. They listened intently as the speaker rose to his feet.

III. OMNISCIENT

One other method by which to tell a story is the omniscient point of view. In this method, the author knows all. He not only reports on the activities of the characters, but he editorializes about their character traits, their inner feelings, their motives. In fact, dealing with the subconscious is the main factor of this point of view. A story of this type is told in the third person too. Examples are:

A. Even he didn't know the reason for doing it.

B. His active mind was planning, scheming.

The Book Report

For a long time, the recognized purpose of a book report has not been so much a source of information as it has been a means of encouraging the reading of a particular work or another of the same topic or by the same author. There are many factors which have made book reporting a dull, ineffective task.

1. Students are required to read material for which they have inadequate ability or a lack of interest.
2. A traditional book report is required, most of which consists of a poorly organized summary of events in the story.
3. More stress is placed on the method than on the motive or the end results.

The primary aims of a book report are to interest potential readers of the book under discussion and to stimulate their imaginations, as well as that of the original reader. The acceptable book report stimulates the reader's interest without divulging so much of the story that its effect is lost. The worthwhile book report is more than a summary, more than a listing of the main events.

One of the purposes of the book report is to evaluate the characters in the book, that is, to make comparisons of characters. What are the individual strong and weak points? What are the character flaws or failures? Another consideration is whether or not the character is an integral part of the story. Is he woven inextricably into the overall mesh of the book?

Individual interpretations are intricately woven into the framework of a good report. It must appeal to the listener's or reader's imagination and emotions. Through the development of the report, the reporter gains a deeper insight into his own prejudices and appreciations. Some of the questions which the report should answer are:

1. What emotions were shown in the book?
2. Why did you like or dislike the book?
3. Would you recommend the book to others for reading? Why?
4. What is one main idea expressed in the book?

Related assignments are:

1. Summarize the plot in one paragraph.
2. Read your favorite scene, incident, or description.
3. Write a sequel to the story.
4. Think of another possible title for the book.

CHECK LIST

1. Why do your students read?
2. Are students concerned with improving their own reading skills?
3. Are they adept at scanning and other more advanced reading skills?
4. Are students consciously trying to enlarge their vocabularies?
5. Do you use oral reading to stimulate interest in the reading program?
6. Are your evaluations really learning techniques?
7. How much do students know about the mechanics of literature, plot, etc.?
8. Are students able to interest others in reading, thus making reading more contagious?

11

An Individualized Reading Program

BROADEN READING TASTES

Children should read a wide variety of material. Their reading may range from newspapers and magazines to *Ripley's Believe It or Not* to Steinbeck's *The Pearl*. They should be encouraged to explore the library thoroughly to find a wide variety of interesting reading material.

Even the slow reader can gain a wealth of knowledge from general geography and science books, which have a minimum of text material and rely mostly on pictures.

Many teachers designate a minimum of 15 minutes each week from the language arts period for individual library work. The students thus become familiar with the library at the elementary level, and as they reach junior high and senior high school, both library research and browsing in the library are practices which are carried out naturally and easily.

Besides the books found in the typical elementary classroom library, such books as the following should be included for reading:

THE SEA AROUND US (Rachel Carson)

Some students may only study the pictures and read the short accompanying descriptions, but even this much reading will justify its inclusion in the classroom library.

Such short intriguing sections as the discussion of the Sargasso Sea, with its strange plant and animal life, about which so many tales have been told, will interest many students. In some cases, though, it may be necessary for the teacher to point out certain parts of books which will have the most interest for them, or which apply to some other area of study.

If at all possible, allow the student to discover these interesting reading experiences for himself, through the index, cross references, from the card catalogue or through other means.

KON-TIKI (Thor Heyerdahl)

Kon-Tiki is also a book about the sea which often attracts a great deal of interest in the elementary grades. Here, too, most editions contain a large number of pictures, accompanied by short, easily understood descriptions.

The exciting chapter "To the South Sea Islands" is a favorite among students who do not wish to read the entire account of Heyerdahl's adventure.

BIOGRAPHY:

For the avid readers of biography, *Out of My Life and Thought*, Albert Schweitzer, *Twenty Years at Hull House*, Jane Addams, *Up from Slavery*, G. W. Carver, *The Story of My Life*, Helen Keller, and *The Making of an American*, Jacob A. Riis, are interesting possibilities for reading.

Such books as *Travels with Charley*, John Steinbeck, which is partly autobiographical, is a book which would satisfy many young readers' tastes. This, too, is the type of book which teachers can very effectively adapt to a geography or social studies class. For instance, Steinbeck's colorful descriptions of various states and their scenic areas give the reader a much clearer picture of the true nature of these areas than does a matter-of-fact geography book description. The teacher may wish to select certain portions of this or a similar book and read it orally to the class.

Parts of Carl Sandburg's "Lincoln" books can be used very effectively in the same way.

400 Notable Americans, Richard B. Morris, is a handy reference source of biographies which should also be a part of the elementary classroom library. Short biographical sketches of the presidents, writers, artists, composers, reformers, and explorers are only a few of the entries in the book. While invaluable as a reference book, it is also a highly readable information book.

Another type of book is the one which places the student in the participant role. A high-interest book which does this very well is *Stop, Look, and Write,* Leavitt and Sohn. It is made up almost entirely of eye-catching and provocative pictures. The students are asked to observe, really see, the pictures, and then write their impressions and descriptions of what they have seen. Models, which in themselves have value for the young reader, also make up a part of the book.

Selective Reading

There is no particular virtue in reading some types of books in their entirety. For instance, some children will undoubtedly wish to read only one story from an anthology of short stories, while others may wish to read several.

In study, only small excerpts are usually read at one time from reference books. Even adults seldom read every word in a newspaper. They are selective, and read only those parts which are of interest to them.

We should not, therefore, except in reading a single story, be concerned that every book a child starts to read be

read completely. Even with novels, the child would be unusual if he did not occasionally read a few pages of a book
and then lay it aside. Eventually, when he is ready for it, he
may again pick it up and read it, or he may decide to spend
his time reading something which to him is more worthwhile.

Oral Reading by the Students

Throughout the entire curriculum, student oral reading
can be effectively utilized. Students may choose short story
selections from various sources and read them to the class.
Since most classes are too large to allow for every student
to read an entire story, make use of the tape recorder. Students record their selections independently, thus providing
material for independent listening. The teacher should record as many stories as possible for student listening. If
possible, one story per day should be provided for them.
Many very good literary selections can be read aloud in less
than fifteen minutes. Occasionally you may wish to read very
short selections such as Aesop's fables, short mythological
tales, or high-interest short hero stories.

The separate section in student notebooks for annotated
bibliographies should also be used for short sketches concerning the author and the story. The student notebook is
the student's responsibility and the student should do this
work independently.

A good listening exercise is to have students read their
own selections. This activity can teach responsibility in
speaking. Stress that it is the speaker's duty to make the listener want to give his full attention to what is being read
and that it is the listener's duty to analyze the speaker ob-
jectively and to be an attentive listener.

Oral Reading by the Teacher

There are many reasons why oral reading by the teacher
to the students is valuable.

1. It improves listening skills.
2. It allows you to present excellent pieces of literature to students.
3. All can share in the same literary experience.
4. It provides an opportunity for discussion.
5. It can create a real interest in literature.

Student interest should generally dictate what you should read. One of the main purposes of oral reading is to broaden students' knowledge and interest in literature. This can be accomplished by reading many different types of literature; e.g., Indian lore, hero stories, adventure stories, etc. By reading a few minutes each day to the student, an impressive number of books and stories can be read during a year. Always provide time for discussion of the selections. Much can be gained through well-directed discussion of literature.

What to Read

The following four books are suitable for oral reading by the teacher or for reading by the entire class.

WINTER THUNDER (Mari Sandoz)

Winter Thunder is a good selection for the intermediate grades. It examines man against the forces of nature. The protagonist, man, is represented by a teacher and her pupils lost in a snowstorm. This is a story which children enjoy immensely. It has just the right amount of anxiety and adventure to make it a good story for children.

In this story, man survives the forces of nature. The story does not have a fairy-tale ending, but it is a fulfilling story in that man has defied nature and has ultimately emerged stronger in character.

Since this is a short, high interest level story, children enjoy hearing it read aloud. Such reading aloud by the teacher offers more opportunities for class discussion. Some discussion questions for this book are:

1. What human characteristics of the small group in the story were responsible for their survival?
2. Do you think the characters were changed in any way by the story?

THE BIG WAVE (Pearl Buck)

This, too, is a small book, but it is one of those timeless stories which can be read by all ages with equal enjoyment. The story has an oriental setting, and it takes place near the sea. The characters are lifelike, and every aspect of the story is believable.

The Big Wave is a good story for this age group. One of the high points of the story occurs when Jiya has to make a decision to accept the old man's offer of a new life in the palace, a good education, etc., or the simple life of his father and the other fishermen.

Discussion Questions

1. Would you have made the same decision as Jiya?
2. Why did the old gentleman make the offer to Jiya?
3. Is life really stronger than death, as the story suggests?

THE ISLAND OF THE BLUE DOLPHINS (Scott O'Dell)

The Island of the Blue Dolphins is a superior book, and every elementary student should have the experience of reading it or of having it read to him. It is an excellent story for fourth, fifth, or sixth graders. The main character is a girl who lives an enchanting, though lonely, life on an island. It also has a unique and interesting ending. Children remember this story for a long time.

Discussion Questions

1. Was_____really lonely on the island?
2. Do you think she was happier before or after her rescue?

OLD RAMON (Jack Schaefer)

Old Ramon is a story of simple adventure and of a boy's outdoor education given him by the title character. This is not a high adventure story, but it is a moving account of how a boy and an old man spend their summer together.

Discussion Questions

1. Which of the old man's characteristics made you like him?
2. What are some of the things the boy learned during the summer?
3. Why was Old Ramon satisfied to live the life he led?
4. Why wasn't money important to Old Ramon?

INDIVIDUALIZING THE READING PROGRAM

What is to be done with the five or six expert readers in a reading class, who are bored with much of the material being read by the average students, and who can read the material in half the time allotted? What is to be done with the average reader who does not take the responsibility for individual reading? What is to be done with the non-reader?

One solution to the above problems is to use rigid grouping. Each group reads at its own speed. Another is to use flexible grouping within a classroom. In the case of many classes, due to limited space, facilities, etc., rigid grouping is simply not possible.

The following plan is a good one to use in either of the above situations. It can also be used for the average and below average reader, whether or not rigid grouping is utilized.

In addition to other class work and specified assignments, each student is given a manila folder which contains reading cards. Some of the cards which may be included in the folders are:

a. A list of adventure books
b. A list of biographies
c. General fiction
d. Books by famous authors

Each card has space for indicating when the book was completed, as well as blanks for listing any other books by the same author or books of the same type which students read during the period.

The students are not asked to read all three of the selections on each card. The three titles are given to provide the students with a choice. In some cases, however, the students choose to read all of the selections listed. When they are finished with a card, they simply ask for another one.

e. A list of short stories by various authors and of varying length
f. Magazine articles of high interest

Students are encouraged to keep newspaper clippings concerning authors, book reviews, etc. These are mounted on a stiff backing and kept as a reference.

As soon as several of the students have read the same story, book, or magazine article, the students have a loosely organized discussion of the story.

The folder method of teaching students to read individually is successful because it is a means of teaching students to organize and keep a record of their reading material. They have guidelines to follow, but the ingenious student is also allowed to make his own selections.

A BOOK LIST FOR ELEMENTARY STUDENTS

Five Little Peppers (Margaret Sidney)
The Laura Ingles Wilder Books
Hans Brinker (Mary Mapes Dodge)
Boy of the Desert (Eunice Tietjen)
Golden Gate (Valenti Anglo)
Florence Nightingale (Irene Cooper Willis)
The Microbe Man, A Life of Pasteur for Young People (Eleanor Doorly)
The Hobbit (J. R. Tolkien)
The White Stag (Kate Seredy)
Boy's Life of Edison (William H. Meadowcroft)
Davy Crockett (Constance Rourke)
Adventures of Pinocchio (Carlo Collodi)
Jungle Books (Rudyard Kipling)
The Wind in the Willows (Kenneth Grahame)
Uncle Remus Stories (Joel Chandler Harris)
The Cat Who Went to Heaven (Elizabeth Coatsworth)
The Curious Lobster (Richard W. Hatch)
The Wonderful Adventures of Nils (Selma Lagerlof)
Bambi (Felix Salten)
Smoke the Cowhorse (Will James)
Black Beauty (Anna Sewell)
Call of the Wild (Jack London)
Stickeen (John Muir)
Rascal (Sterling North)
The Children of Odin (Padraic Colum)
King of the Golden River (John Ruskin)
Rootabago Stories (Carl Sandburg)
Just So Stories (Rudyard Kipling)
Treasure Island (Robert L. Stevenson)
Time Machine (H. G. Wells)
The Big Wave (Pearl S. Buck)

Lad: A Dog (Albert Payson Terhune)
Banner in the Sky (James Ramsey Ullman)
The Storycatcher (Mari Sandoz)
Christmas of the Phonograph Records (Mari
    Sandoz
Winter Thunder (Mari Sandoz)
Robinson Crusoe (Daniel Defoe)
Book of Ten Great Mysteries (Edgar Allan Poe)
The Light in the Forest (Conrad Richter)
Prince and the Pauper (Mark Twain)
Swiss Family Robinson (Johann Wyss)
Caddie Woodlawn (Carol Ryrie Brink)
Lassie Come Home (Eric Knight)
My Friend Flicka (Mary O'Hara)
Call It Courage (Armstrong Sperry)
Homer Price (Robert McCloskey)
Secret of the Andes (Ann N. Clark)
Heidi (Johanna Spyri)
The Yearling (Marjorie Kinnan Rawlings)
Big Red (Jim Kjelgaard)
20,000 Leagues Under the Sea (Jules Verne)
Penrod (Booth Tarkington)
Black Stallion (Walter Farley)
Ben and Me (Robert Lawson)
Island of the Blue Dolphins (Scott O'Dell)
Little Britches (Ralph Moody)
Pecos Bill and Lightning (Leigh Peck)
Lantern in Her Hand (Bess Aldrich)

REFERENCE BOOKS FOR THE ELEMENTARY CLASSROOM LIBRARY

Ripley's Believe It or Not
The Sea Around Us
Bartlett's Quotations
The World Almanac
Stop, Look, and Write

400 Notable Americans
Facts About the Presidents
Sould's Dictionary of English Synonyms
Who's Who in America
The U.S. Book of Facts, Statistics, and Information
Great Quotations
The Complete Reference Handbook

BOOKS OF POETRY

Complete Poems of Robert Frost (Frost)
The Pocket Book of Ogden Nash (Nash)
You Come Too: Favorite Poems for Young Readers (Frost)
Salt Water Ballads (John Masefield)
Poems (Rachel Field)
The American Songbag (Carl Sandburg)

12

Teaching the Importance of Research Skills

To a large extent the success or failure of a language arts program can be judged accurately by analyzing the types of questions that are asked: (1) Those asked by the teacher which require a reply by the students; (2) Those asked by the students which require an answer either from the teacher or from a student who is making a report, involved in a discussion, or in some other way responsible for an answer to a question which has been asked; (3) Those raised jointly by the teacher and students as a means of setting goals for a new learning experience; (4) Those questions which require individual research and experimentation.

Teacher-Originated Questions

Well-planned questions interjected by the teacher into a class may mean the difference between a learning and a non-learning situation. Good questions make students think and the differences between thinking and merely remembering are pronounced. Thought questions ask for comparisons, and they are exploratory questions which begin with how and why. If the student confronts this type of question, he must become involved, forming opinions and drawing conclusions.

Objective-type questions—true-false, matching, fill-in-the-blank, etc.—have a part in evaluating how much of the subject matter of a unit or of a lesson the student can recall. But these questions do not require real thought or origination of new ideas; they demand only that the student remember what he has heard and studied before.

The purposes of the teacher-originated thought questions are many. First, thought questions make students more independent in learning, making them less afraid to respond with opinions and new ideas. Without fears, related to responses, they soon discover new depths of thought and expression within themselves. The response to a thought question tells the teacher what a student really has learned, not merely what facts he can recall from a short time before. One other important reason for asking these questions is that in order to consistently form worthwhile opinions and ideas, students must read and listen with a great deal of care and interpretation.

The Students Ask Questions

The type of questions students ask in a literature class, for example, is an important indication of the value of the class. Are the students interested in the characters in a story for understanding people and situations which relate to themselves or are they interested only in superficial factors and qualities related to the characters? The nature of their questions will often reveal the answer.

Preliminary Questions

An important questioning situation is preliminary questioning—before a lesson, before reading a story, before a report. What value is there in reading a story if the reader has absolutely no purpose in reading it? What can be gained from a report or from a unit of study if no goals have been set? Probably nothing of real value will be gained. Goals for study are indispensable and they seem most effective if they are in the form of questions.

Preliminary questions should be developed by the students with the teacher's guidance. The old method of placing a list of goals in the planbook for the teacher's use only was dropped long ago. The student must have goals if he is to accomplish any real learning, and certainly if he is to learn according to any long-range plan.

In the case of reading, it may be necessary to skim the material before goals in the form of questions are listed. When a social studies or science unit is to be studied, for instance, a short preliminary discussion should be conducted to familiarize students with what can be learned in the unit so they can form their opinion of what *they* want to learn rather than what the teacher wants them to learn.

Questions Related to the Student

To give students first-hand experience with questioning and problem solving, ask questions which are closely related to them and incorporate similar questions asked by the students into the curriculum. These questions should be those which relate to real problems and which need an answer given by students. These are problems which should be solved by following these steps:

1. Select a pertinent problem which is within the scope of an elementary student's ability.
2. Formulate a conjecture or hypothesis.
3. Develop a plan of procedure.
4. Accumulate information.
5. Process and interpret the information.
6. Report the findings to the class.

Some problems which elementary students should learn to solve may be patterned after the following:

1. Which student magazine would best meet the needs of the class?

This question establishes a goal closely related to the students, and it can be solved by using the steps in problem solving. Arriving at an answer to this question will involve close scrutiny of several student newspapers and magazines, discussions with several students, conducted to determine which are most widely read, which are read mostly for enjoyment, which are read for their scientific information, which are read because of current news value, which are of the most value to the greatest number of students.

2. How can we enlarge our classroom paperback library?

Solving problems of this type offers an excellent opportunity for teaching concepts related to economics—raising and handling money, public relations, gaining support for the idea, etc.

3. What clothing regulations should we have for our class?

This type of question is so closely related to the student that few will be indifferent to it.

OPINION QUESTIONS   Extremely opinionated remarks are to be avoided by students in answering opinion questions; however, honest expression of opinion does have a place in the elementary school. Here is an outline of conditions and procedures which serve to elicit opinions from students:

1. The students are already aware of the problem.
2. The entire class has been asked individually to gather as much information on the problem as possible by reading, through listening to radio and television broadcasts, and by asking well-directed questions of the student to help him in forming an opinion.
3. The teacher finds a short interpretive editorial or news article from a student newspaper and reads it to the class.

4. Each student with a different opinion expresses it in the following manner:
   a. In the form of an opinion, not a fact:
      (1) I think, I believe. . . .
      (2) I like. . . .
      (3) It seems to me. . . .
   b. Avoid statements similar to the following:
      (1) . . . is the craziest idea I've ever heard.
      (2) I don't know how anyone could possibly believe. . . .
5. Each differing opinion is recorded for future reference.
6. After all of the opinions have been heard and recorded, a discussion follows to determine what facts, if any, can be found to support the opinion.

Research Must Begin Early

Research in the elementary school? To what extent can it be used in elementary classes? Of what value is it? What procedures should be followed?

If children are really to learn, research is necessary, even in the elementary school. Let's take the areas of writing and speaking as examples. Few elementary. students in intermediate grades, when giving an information speech or information written report, can simply give it from experience. That is, it is impossible for them to speak or write without at least a limited amount of research, and say anything that is of value to the audience. This does not mean that the research must be comprehensive in the beginning, but it should at least be thorough enough to explode myths which so often cloud a subject in a child's mind.

This section on research is based on the premise that one of the principal goals of education is a knowledge of man and his world. We must conclude that a working interest and an open attitude toward learning is imperative. We must recognize that both facts and ideas play a vital role in the educational process.

One method of fostering learning and whetting the student's thirst for knowledge is to intersperse interesting and worthwhile facts and ideas into every area of the curriculum. It will not be necessary for the teacher to simply relate these facts and ideas to the students, but it will be more effective if he can help the students to discover these by themselves.

This practice need not and should not be a dull mechanical presentation, but rather a spontaneous attempt to make learning infectious. Sparks of interest will ultimately lead to student self-direction.

According to Webster, "A fact is what has really happened or is the case; truth; reality." An idea is ". . . any conception existing in the mind as the result of mental apprehension or activity." Facts as well as ideas must be taught in the classroom. Facts and ideas are interdependent, and together they must be woven into the fabric of a good education. This idea, certainly a part of the language arts, extends into the other subject areas as well. Problem solving, research, and scientific discovery depend on the effective utilization of facts.

THE REFERENCE BOOK   Avoid whenever possible research assignments which tend to create unfavorable attitudes. Reference books should be thought of as aids to learning, and not as meaningless additions to the library. An example of an inhibiting exercise with reference books is the typical long list of historical events for which students must supply the missing dates.

In its broadest sense, reference material is any source that provides necessary information for a topic under study. Newspapers, magazines, recordings, etc. are all reference sources and they should not be overlooked when research is being done. Not to be overlooked by elementary students are more specialized reference materials such as *Who's Who* and specialized encyclopedias.

The Why, the What, and the How of the Research Question

We are now considering language arts in a very broad sense. Some further premises assumed for this chapter are:

1. That any subject taught in elementary school is dependent on language arts skills and concepts.
2. That unless the subject matter is filled with interest and meaning for the student, little real learning will take place.
3. That students will have already acquired basic skills for using reference books before this chapter is considered.
4. That the serious search for knowledge really begins in the language arts.

It is because of the fourth premise that this chapter is written. Elementary students are naturally curious about their environment. Your job is to exploit and encourage the constant search for the why, what, when, and how. It is the student who has been repeatedly thwarted in his learning efforts by a dearth of direction or an abundance of misdirection who adopts a lethargic attitude toward learning.

The Purposes of the Research Question

1. To broaden the child's field of knowledge.
2. To whet his appetite for learning.
3. To stimulate interest.
4. To provide meaningful practice with reference books.
5. To cause him to think clearly and to draw conclusions.

One of the advantages of research is that much information which has no definite place in any of the established curriculum areas can be introduced. Another is that it stimulates students' curiosity, which serves as the motivating factor. One other purpose is that it adds interest and color to the entire educational program. Your method of presentation in this area will vary from that used by any other teacher. But some suggestions should be helpful:

1. Be sure the material is on the level of most of the students. (Remember that students' abilities are very frequently underestimated.)
2. Evaluate the assignment in terms of interest.
3. Have necessary reference books available.
4. Make the assignment as clear as possible.
5. Research should usually not be made compulsory in the elementary grades. If students don't take an active interest in the research questions, one of the above elements has probably been omitted. In other words, students' interest is your judge of your methods and materials.

The Incidental Research Question

Suppose your class has just completed a scientific experiment. The students are cleaning their instruments in the sink when one alert student asks why the whirlpool created in the draining sink is revolving clockwise. Most science teachers could launch a lengthy discussion on the Coriolis effect and many students would be intrigued with the explanation, but why not utilize this opportunity for individual research? Suggest that students try to find the answer for themselves. If you feel that some hints are necessary, give them the word Coriolis, and then let them proceed independently. Do not insist that all the students bring the answer to class the next day, but let them take the initiative. Don't be frustrated if only a few students find the answer to this type of question at first. Perhaps more practice is needed with the reference books, but it is more likely that the main problem is closer to the student. He has not yet generated enough "steam," or he may simply not have the ability to tackle this type of problem independently. For the student who has the ability to arrive at answers independently, try to stimulate and maintain interest in the incidental research question.

Other questions which can be used in the above manner are:

1. *Why do wild animals seldom die of old age?*
   (Students should arrive at the conclusion that when an animal weakens in his natural habitat, it is vulnerable to predators and is thus not usually permitted to die naturally.)

2. *What is the average length of time required for a full-size lumber tree to develop?*
   (When consulting different reference books, students may be confronted with more than one possible answer. The question of reliability is then raised, and students should learn to cope with it. Such factors as date of publication, amount of research done in the compilation of the reference book, and its reliability in the past should be considered.)

3. *Why is glass considered a poor conductor of electricity?*
   (After consulting various science references, students should arrive at the conclusion that glass and many other materials are considered poor conductors because they hold on to their electrons, thus slowing the passage of the electric current.)

4. *Compare the amount of water on the earth now with the amount thousands of years ago.*
   (This concept may be difficult for many students to grasp, but through the conventional methods of research, they should conclude that there is the same amount of water on the earth and in its atmosphere now as there was thousands of

years ago. It is constantly being recycled and it continually shifts positions, but there is no way for it to escape the earth or its atmosphere. Water can never be used up.)

The Question Which Is a Supplement to Other Learning

1. Used in visual areas—bulletin boards, etc.
2. In oral discussions
3. Individual research and group assimilation, class file, notebook, etc.

A great deal of classroom information can best be presented in the form of bulletin board displays or in some other type of classroom research display. Too, it may become part of the classroom file or notebook, to be used for future reference. Work in this area is most effective if it is voluntary. Seeing and reading and voluntarily answering questions raised on the classroom bulletin board is, for many students, one more source of interesting stimulation.

We must recognize the fact that some students will never take an active interest in a display such as these mentioned, and others will have only a passing interest. But, just as no text or classroom lesson can meet the needs of all of the students, no display will have the same value for the entire class. This, however, is not a valid reason for omitting such a display. It should not occupy the primary display board, in most cases, but a special area should be set aside for frequent, well-chosen research ideas.

Too frequently the curriculum suffers because the goal is to meet the needs of most of the students with the same materials. This method is just not acceptable in many cases. A parallel can be drawn to a newspaper editorial. Many editors realize, and numerous polls indicate, that the editorial page of a newspaper is read by only a small percentage of the overall audience, but they continue to print the editorials because they feel that an interested audience of even that size is important.

If three main flexible intelligence groups are given special attention in the classroom, it is only appropriate that special displays be maintained. Intra-group work in setting up the displays can minimize the teacher-time used to set them up. Many teachers use the team approach—one half of the students in each group develop and display research material for the other half of the group.

Questions Which May Be Used in This Category Are:

1. Place the following three early civilizations in order of their development: (fertile crescent, Hwang Valley, Yangtze Valley)
2. The word *Europe* means_____and the word *Asia* means_____.
3. Why was the starling introduced into the United States? (Because of an attempt to cultivate all of the birds found in Shakespeare's works.)

Solving the Problem with Experimentation Supplemented by Research

Recent studies of the Soviet Union's educational system have revealed that while students there could recall facts prodigiously, they had a great deal of trouble in problem solving. The study also revealed that the majority of students were unable to provide self-direction and motivation. Our society requires problem-solvers, however.

In this type of research question, students should be given enough latitude to work imaginatively. Most of these questions should be presented as enrichment. Some examples which may be used in science are:

    I. The soil test:

        MATERIALS: Three types of soil: clay, loam, sandy.

        PROCEDURE: Add one type of soil to each glass

of water and let the glasses sit for 15 minutes or longer.

QUESTIONS: Why didn't the clay particles settle to the bottom of the beaker? How can we clear the water? (by adding alum)

II. Find the air capacity of a unit of soil:

PROCEDURE: Weigh the soil.

Pour water into the beaker until the soil is completely saturated.

Weigh the saturated soil.

Find the difference between the dry and wet weight of the soil.

III. By using a perpetual calendar, find out how many days you have lived. (Don't forget leap years.)

FOR THE LESSON   One other type of research question is that which is a direct result of a classroom lesson or a part of the preparation for a lesson. To be successful with this popular type of problem, students must have a good working knowledge of research materials and techniques. The good student will soon recognize that understanding of research materials can best come through use. Too, students should be encouraged to develop the habit of checking information which they hear and read for accuracy.

Original Research

Original research may take the form of one of the following:

I. Weather Charts: Compiling weather information in a variety of forms.

II. Soil Tests: Many simple soil experiments can be conducted by the elementary student.

III. Study of genetics:

a. Each child compiles a family tree—making it as complete as possible.
b. Each child charts the following information concerning his family:
   (1) hair color
   (2) color of eyes
   (3) complexion
   (4) height
   (5) weight
c. Students then, using this information, determine which traits are dominant. They should rely heavily on reference books as a test of the reliability of their findings.

IV. Probability: Drop a coin a hundred times to determine the range of probability.

V. Word Usage: Analyze paragraphs to determine which words are used most. Students should chart their conclusions.

VI. Word Association: Give spontaneous word association quizzes. This exercise should consist of several ordinary words for which the rest of the class supplies the first word which comes to mind. This experiment may encompass several classes to provide a wide sampling. Although this exercise does not have great practical value, it provides excellent experience in basic research.

The Notebook and Research

Students will benefit most from research if they keep a record of information which they have located and organized from various sources. The three ring notebook is the best format for the personal reference book. A great deal of time can be saved if important facts and ideas are categorized by the student. The student should be encouraged to record only information which will have value for *him*. Information should be put in brief form under the proper heading. The margin may be used to indicate sources.

One important purpose of the notebook is to provide an outlet for individual work. Students use the notebook to organize research on some particular topic for which they have specific interest. As research is being done, information can conveniently be recorded on file cards.

Honest Statistics

Using statistics correctly and honestly when doing research is an art which must be acquired by the serious student. In the modern age of computers in which statistics are given a very prominent position, discriminate use of statistics is paramount to valuable research. Take, for instance, this example. A small European country has been producing almost no petroleum. Then, however, two new petroleum wells are brought into production. Statistics for that year may show a 50 percent increase in production. This is an impressive figure until one considers amount rather than percentage.

Similarly, country A's production of iron ore may increase by only a few thousands of tons. This rise in production may increase the percentage by ten points. The production of iron ore in country B may be increased by millions of tons but, because of their past record of production, the percentage may increase by only five points.

Discriminate use of population statistics is also as important as it is difficult. Population figures, usually based on ten year censuses, are in many cases necessarily based on estimation. This means that many population figures are actually much in error at the time of first publication. The student who wishes to use these figures must take this fact into consideration. He must also adjust the figures to compensate for the ten year period between censuses.

CHECK LIST

1. Are the teacher-originated questions open-ended?
2. Do the students' questions reflect an interest in and an increasing knowledge of literature?
3. Do the opinion questions reflect logical thinking?
4. Does research begin early in your language arts program?
5. How adept are students at using research books?
6. Are incidental research questions improving your language arts program?
7. Are worthwhile questions supplementing your language arts program?
8. How effectively are students using independent research as a learning device?

13

Using the Library
to Strengthen
the Language Arts Program

Learning to use the library involves much more than an annual or semi-annual class trip or tour of the school or public library. It involves more than one or two summary research assignments or the perusal of two or three reference sources. These constitute only the beginning of a sound library and study program.

Teaching library use is an important part of the elementary curriculum.

Yes, it is important—it is indispensable to good study habits, to responsibility for learning, and to developing good study habits for research. Many of these skills will be used throughout the child's life. It is important, then, that they be learned well.

Library skills are so important that they should be introduced no later than the fourth grade, and if possible, even in lower grades. The number of high school students who cannot actually use the library in completing a single research assignment is simply astounding. Many of these students do not lack the ability. They lack the skill and interest.

In one high school class, the students, in being introduced to a unit on the library, confounded their teacher by looking in the front of the textbook for the index, registering no knowledge of the table of contents, and by asking "What's that?" when the teacher mentioned the word *Almanac*. Such ignorance is without excuse. Any student who has enough competence to attend school and to do at least passable work can learn to use the library effectively and can develop an interest in library research.

Students first need to become acquainted with the library. This means not only an initial explanatory and exploratory tour of the library, but repeated visits in the company of the teacher until the students finally begin to develop skill in using the library.

THE INITIAL VISIT   Many students will have been in a library before they ever attend a single day of school. Indeed, in some cases the third or fourth grade student who has not been in at least one other library, besides the one in the school, is rare.

In some schools where a severe cultural lag is felt, many students have never been in a library. The school library may be inadequate or nonexistent, but in such cases the problem is not insurmountable. The teacher, at least, in almost all cases has access to a library. He can check out materials and bring them to the classroom as a last resort. Certainly this much exposure to reference materials is better than none at all. Fortunately, however, such extremes are few.

If, however, a good library is available, a great deal can be accomplished on the first visit. The important point at this stage of the students' learning is to try to develop interest in using the library. The teacher may map out a route in the library for the first visit:

1. Go to the telephone directories and find the

telephone number listing of a friend or relative of one of the class members who lives in a city some distance away.

2. Tour the newspaper room. Read the first-hand account of the first firing of a manned space vehicle, the bombing of Pearl Harbor, the assassination of President Kennedy, or read about an event which occurred in your own city some time before.

3. Visit the reserve reference book section. Locate an almanac and find out how much working time is required for buying a loaf of bread or a pair of shoes.

4. Use a gazetteer to confirm the population of your city.

5. Find an interesting page in a current magazine and reproduce it on the copy machine.

6. By using the card catalogue, locate and check out a book for class reading.

7. Use the latest edition of *Who's Who* to find interesting information about the president or some other famous person.

8. Spend a few minutes browsing in the children's section of the library.

NOW LET'S USE IT   Now that students have been introduced to several facets of the library, actual research can begin. It is necessary to keep in mind, though, that a great deal of library practice must be carried out before maximum benefit from the library will be reached. The practice should be short, yet not without interest for the student.

It is best to begin the practice with not more than two or three research questions per week. The one or more reference sources used can be brought to the classroom and passed around the room, each student working individually. Examples for this type of research follow:

1. What is the population of Sydney, Australia?

2. When was television invented?

3. Who currently holds the record for the mile run?

To keep interest high, have library treasure hunts. Each side is given a work assignment to complete. The assignment may include five to ten questions which require the use of several references: the almanac, the card catalogue, the unabridged dictionary, etc. Don't forget to use newspapers and magazines in these assignments.

LEARNING IN THE LIBRARY

Library practice serves more than one purpose. It not only teaches students locational skills, but the students can learn many new and interesting bits of information as part of their library practice. The importance of making library practice interesting cannot be overstressed.

One brilliant science student traces his first interest in bacteriology to a library research question. The question was, "How high in the atmosphere can bacteria be found?" After a rather lengthy search, he quoted one source as giving the answer of approximately four miles. In the search for the answer to this single question, though, he discovered several other bacteriological concepts.

Practice in the Library

WHO'S WHO

Find the entry for the president of the United States and rewrite the entry in paragraph form, giving entire words instead of abbreviations and adding words to give the entry more interest. Encourage students to use the table of abbreviations at the front of the book.

Have students use *Who's Who* to locate information concerning the author of the book the class is currently reading. They might answer such questions as "How old was

Pearl S. Buck when *The Big Wave* was published?" "How many other books has Pearl S. Buck written?"

Ask questions which relate to the students:

STATISTICAL ABSTRACT OF THE UNITED STATES

1. How many fourth, fifth, or sixth grade students are there in the U.S.?
2. What is the population density of your state?
3. How many cattle are in the U.S.?
4. How many eating places are in the U.S.?
5. How much did the population of (your town) increase/decrease during the past decade?

ALMANAC

1. What is the elevation of (your town)?
2. Give the five main languages, in order, now spoken in the world.

Other questions you might ask:

1. Which of the Balkan capitals is said to be the most attractive?
2. Which is probably older—Niagara Falls or Mammoth Cave?
3. When did Genghis Khan die?
4. How much work time is required to buy one pound of bread?
5. Who wrote *Island in the Sun*?
6. What does the word *hemidemisemiquaver* mean?
7. Find and write one of Mark Twain's quotations.
8. Who said "Our Republic and its press will rise or fall together"?
9. What is the meaning of the word *narwhal*?
10. Why are the deepest parts of the ocean called the *Hadal Zones*?

11. When was Harper Lee born?
12. What is the name of the current which encircles the Antarctic continent?
13. How many people visited our national parks last year?
14. How many people were immigrants to the U.S. last year?

Other Activities

1. Make drawings or collages which relate to a story or book the class is reading. Write a description of the picture or a short narrative to go along with the picture. The good student should write this narrative in the same style as the original selection. If the selection was poetry, some students may want to write a few lines of original poetry.
2. Organize panel discussions on various topics. *Example:*

TOPIC: LIFE IN THE SEA

Student A: Small Plant Life
Student B: Large Plants in the Sea
Student C: Small Sea Animals
Student D: Giants of the Sea
Student E: Oddities in the Sea
Student F: The Ocean Floor
Student G: Man and the Ocean

The chairman of the group first gives an overview of the material to be covered by the panel. Each of the other students gives an interesting report of his topic, using examples and visual aids where possible.

The chairman gives a brief summation of the material covered in the reports, to help the listener relate the various reports to each other.

The audience is then allowed to ask the panel questions and to raise interesting points which were not covered by the panel.

3. In the Library. Plan to spend at least 15 minutes of each week in the library, either getting acquanted with reference books, doing research, or reading for fun. Occasionally have a library treasure hunt.

    Example: Each side is given a work assignment to complete. The assignment may include five to ten questions which require the use of several reference books: the almanac, encyclopedias, the card catalogue, the unabridged dictionary, etc. You may wish to make this assignment an individual rather than a group project.

    Don't forget to use newspapers and magazines in this assignment.

4. Construct bulletin boards but omit the title. Designate certain students to originate, assimilate, and mount an imaginative caption for the board.

5. Each student should keep a manila folder as a file of material read during the year. This includes book lists of possible titles for reading, lists of books read, current newspaper and magazine clippings of contemporary poets and authors, etc.

6. Rewrite directions, current prose in newspaper articles, and everyday conversation in Shakespearean style, Sherlock Holmes style, or in the style used in the King James Version of the Bible.

7. Write definitions. Write a definition of simple words like book, water, fence, tall, car, money, etc. These definitions should be written in dictionary style. Stress conciseness, brevity, and clarity. After you have written your definition, compare it with the dictionary entry. More practice will probably be needed in defining abstract words such as criticism, difficult, thought, idea, honesty, etc.

8. Write a longer definition of a word. Choose a word like friendship, companion, celebration, suggestion, and write a one paragraph definition. Check the paragraph for

mechanical errors and misstatements. Place yourself in the position of someone who has never before heard the word. Is its meaning clear?

9. Write a persuasive paragraph. Use letters written to the editors of various publications as examples. Be courteous, yet firm. Don't make rash statements. Avoid clichés. Support your ideas and charges. Explain fully your suggestions.

10. A Class Report. When you are teaching students to write reports, use the group approach: Divide the report into sub-topics. Each group works on a different sub-topic.

11. Give students a list of sentences, all of which use a single objectionable word or phrase. Let them rewrite the sentences, eliminating the objectionable part. Examples follow:

  A. Eliminate "there" from the following sentences, making them more direct and more interesting.
    1. There are many pine trees in the park.
       (The park has many pine trees.)
    2. There will be no club meeting tomorrow.
       (The club will not have a meeting tomorrow.)
    3. We were there before the coach arrived.
       (We arrived before the coach did.)
    4. His idea is a strange one, but there may be a logical explanation for it.
       (His idea is a strange one, but he may have a logical explanation for it.)

  B. Give students examples of wordy sentences and let them make them more concise.
    1. Suddenly there was the sound of rain on the roof.
       (Suddenly, we heard rain on the roof.)
    2. At midnight there was a weakening of the bridge as a wall of water passed under it.
       (A wall of water weakened the bridge at midnight.)

3. There was a speech by the student representative at the banquet.
   (The student representative made a speech at the banquet.)

C. Eliminate the personal pronouns I and me from the following sentences:
   1. I don't see how anyone could disagree with the council's plan.
   2. To me, James Thurber was one of the most humorous American writers of this century.
   3. I could not believe I had heard him correctly.
      (It was hard to believe what he said.)

D. Eliminate the second person pronouns from the following sentences.
   1. After closing the box, you fasten it securely.
   2. You cannot become a fast reader in one day.
      (It takes more than a single day to become a fast reader.)

12. Write an epilog to the book *Big Wave*.

13. When reading a book as a class, individual students select the single main event from each chapter and list them on a large piece of oak tag. This procedure provides the story in capsule form.

14. When the class is reading a book, let the students choose a single quotation from the book and illustrate it with a picture they have drawn or a magazine picture which they have found.

15. Let students find pictures to represent characters in the book. The rest of the class decides how closely the picture represents the character designated.

16. Occasionally place a premium on time, when students are using reference books. For instance, give students one or two research questions and give extra points to the one who finds the correct answer first.

17. Listen to music and express the mood in words.

18. Use the newspaper for writing assignments:
    A different approach to writing adds spice to the

language arts program. One means of diversifying the writing program and thus adding more color to it is to use the newspaper.

The following five newspaper writing assignments provide needed practice, a broadened interest in writing, and improved writing skills in language arts classes.

I. NEWSPAPER HEADLINES AS TITLES FOR CREATIVE WRITING ASSIGNMENTS
Choose unique and interesting newspaper headlines and use them as the basis for a creative writing assignment. Students choose from a list of titles such as the following:
a. Bones Unlock Secret
b. Matter of Life and Death
c. Old Teeth Found
The students develop these headlines into stories. After they have written their stories they compare them with the newspaper version.

II. DEVELOPING A PARAGRAPH
Give students the title and the topic sentence of a high-interest newspaper story. Let them finish the first paragraph. Some students may wish to write several paragraphs.

III. WORDS FROM CONTEXT
Give students a copy of a short newspaper article from which five or six important words have been deleted. Students fill the blanks with appropriate words.

IV. LEARNING TO WRITE GOOD TITLES
Give students copies of high-interest newspaper stories and let them supply concise and appropriate titles.

V. CAPTIONS FOR CARTOONS AND CARICATURES
Mount cartoons for a bulletin board display and let students write their own captions or leg-

ends for them. The original captions are deleted.

19. Observation:

The good writer relies heavily on observation. He concerns himself with main points as well as with details. A quiz similar to the following helps students to analyze their observational skills:

1. Whose picture appears on the fact of the current issue dime?
2. Which traffic sign has the shape of a reversed triangle?
3. What is your postal zip code?
4. Is the first stripe on the U.S. flag red or white?
5. On a clock or watch, is the hour hand mounted above or below the minute hand?
6. How many holes are in the dial of a dial telephone?
7. The star is the symbol for which brand of gasoline?
8. What does the symbol ® represent?
9. What does the symbol © represent?

20. The News Sheet:

Produce a weekly news sheet in your classroom. Assimilate the news in capsule form each week. An editorial committee outlines the format. The class can reproduce enough copies for the entire class.

21. Organization in Writing:

Combine and rewrite the following sentences to make them more interesting and more readable:

I live in a small town.
The town is in North Dakota.
540 people live there.
Some people like to live in small towns.
I prefer larger cities.
Small towns have advantages.
Small towns have disadvantages.
Large towns have advantages.

Large towns have disadvantages.
(Try to think of interesting sentences with which to begin and end your paragraph.)

22. Study the following Confucian saying, then rewrite it in your own words: "Ignorance is the night of the mind, a night without moon or star."

     Students may wish to rewrite the following quotations or give supporting examples for them:
     "If you put a chain around the neck of a slave, the other end fastens itself around your own." (Emerson)
     "One with the law is the majority."   (Coolidge)
     "Colors speak all languages."   (Addison)

POETRY

23. Have students rewrite short poems in paragraph form. The poems used for this assignment should be short, meaningful ones which are of interest to students.

24. Give students a copy of a particular poem and ask them to write the theme or main idea of the poem. The principal ideas should be written in the student's own words.

25. Look for figures of speech in poems—metaphors, similes, etc.

26. Explain the meaning of the word "alliteration" and give the students several examples. (Alliteration is repetition of the same first sound, to give the poem a more rhythmical sound.) Students should then find several examples independently.

27. Let students draw their impressions of the setting of some of the more graphic poems.

28. Silent Communication:

     To illustrate silent communication, make use of the pantomime in your class. Students choose a directive to relay to the class silently, such as "Turn off the lights!", "Clear your desks!", "Erase the blackboard!", "Close the door!", "Answer the telephone!", etc. Outside, experiment with distance signaling. A few outside signal directives are:

A. Lower the flag.
B. Drop to the ground.
C. Turn around.
D. Move backwards.

14

The Continuing Language Arts Program

In the lower elementary grades, the language arts period is divided into segments. One segment is the reading program, another the writing program, and still another the oral skills segment.

However, in the intermediate and upper elementary grades, the pattern changes. The blocked program is usually most successful, beginning in third or fourth grade. In a blocked program, the language arts period is a combination of reading, written skills, oral skills, study skills, library practice, etc.

The longer period allows for a fuller development and more careful teaching of new concepts. Students also have more time for individual and group work.

Set the Atmosphere

The successful language arts period begins in an interesting way. Read a short story, poem, newspaper, or magazine article to the students. This type of a class beginning catches the students' attention immediately. It helps to set the tone of the class, creating a good teacher-student rapport. It also has other benefits. Students can and do learn a great deal from these short capsule periods.

The following class beginnings work well in most classes:

a. Listen to a recording of Robert Frost reading "The Witch of Coos."

b. Develop Vachel Lindsay's "The Congo" chorally, supplying the sound effects.

c. Listen to a recording of the news, then write your own news release.

d. Give a five point dictionary practice.

e. Teach independence through research, good study skills, etc.

It is impossible to conduct a language arts class which will meet all of the needs of all of the students. For this reason, some type of grouping must be carried out.

Advantages of the Longer Class Period

One advantage of the longer language arts program is the opportunity a class has of developing longer assignments. Some of these which can be completed by elementary students are:

a. Write and produce your own play. Since most students enjoy competition, better plays result from group work.

b. Write and produce your own class newspaper.

c. Develop class booklets of creative and free writing booklets.

Developing the Class Work Assignment

A. MAIN EVENTS AND DETAILS

Ask questions which help to reveal the obvious parts of the story. It is often helpful to develop a story on the overhead projector—each student supplying either an appropriate main event or a detail.

B. LISTENING

A good listening activity to be used at this point in the development of the lesson is to read several quotations from the story, letting students recall the speaker.

Also, to improve and evaluate comprehension, read only parts of important statements from the story, letting students finish the statement. You might ask them to complete statements similar to the following:

1. Paul was nearly 8 years old when. . . .
2. Don was made to work so long in the hold that. . . .
3. Not until the last trip, late that evening, did. . . .

C. STUDENTS CHOOSE A BRIEF EXCERPT FROM A GOOD BOOK THEY HAVE READ TO READ TO THE CLASS

Setting Up the Schedule

The following is an outline for a language arts program:

8:30–8:37   Introductory material (above)

8:37–8:47   Oral reading by individual students and choral reading of poems.

(Frequently, after reading a selection silently, reread a section by having each student read a single sentence.) This time can also be used for dramatizations. Let students choose segments of the stories which are made up of conversation and read them as dramatically as possible, acting rather than reading the "he said," "he nodded," sections.

8:47–9:10	Silent reading of new selection
9:10–9:30	Discussion of selection and written development of it. Writing epilogs, new titles, dialog, etc.
9:30–9:40	Spelling and vocabulary practice
9:40–10:00	Creative writing-grammatical concepts, etc.
10:00–10:30	Group and individual library research— Guided group preparation and completion of panel discussions, play writing and production, listening activities, individual reading.

The Language Arts Class Should:

a. Interest the student in learning
b. Teach him the basic language arts skills
c. Teach human relations
d. Increase the knowledge of literature

Now, you are ready for the open-end questions and the discussion questions:

(1) What might have happened if . . . ?
(2) Who was the most . . . ?

SHALL WE TEACH. . . .

Before any unit is introduced into the curriculum, the teacher and the student must be convinced that it has value. Will it meet the needs of the students? Does it rank high on the list of language arts priorities?

Shall We Teach Grammar?

To clarify, grammar involves sentence structure and word relationships. Usage is a term usually applied to colloquial expression, correct word choice, etc. Punctuation, capitals, hyphens, etc. are usually grouped under the heading of mechanics. Grammar, usage, and mechanics are part of every language arts class, regardless of the goals established or the type of organization employed. Grammar is an indispensable element of every language arts class. It may be given other names and old methods may be refuted, but grammar plays a part in all writing and in all speaking. The question, then, is not "Shall we teach grammar?" but "What approach shall we use?"

Before a teacher can successfully teach grammar, he must first have justified to himself the importance of this segment of language arts. He will have to face such problems as the following:

    a. Is grammar important enough to warrant spending large blocks of time in teaching it?

    b. Should it be taught as a separate entity?

    c. How much does the elementary child benefit from the study of grammar?

    d. What about the child who must be retaught and R-E-T-A-U-G-H-T?

    e. How can grammar be taught with meaning?

These are questions which must be considered very carefully before the language arts class can successfully operate. These questions cannot be answered easily. They must be answered differently for each teaching situation. They must be reconsidered frequently to keep the aims of the program current.

Students are expected to know grammar when they enter high school and eventually college, and if they are to learn it, obviously someone must teach it. Admittedly, this is not a very good reason on which to base our teaching, but it is a fact which must be taken into consideration. Why, though, must we make the teaching of grammar a complete bore? And why can't we relate to the child's current needs? The indispensable criterion for teaching grammar is *need*. When the occasion arises for sending real letters, and such an occasion may arise as early as first grade, spend some time actually teaching grammar, for instance.

A fourth, fifth, or sixth grade class may be writing sentences with faulty reference, poor diction, or poor parallelism. It is usually inadvisable to specifically name the error and discuss it at length, but the matter should be attended to, nevertheless. The best method in this case is to present, one at a time, sentences which contain similar errors. Ask students to read the faulty sentences aloud, trying to "pin down" the error. The error is usually more obvious if repeated orally.

Quite often these written errors are ones which the child almost never makes in his oral speech. Sometimes the reverse is true. The student makes oral errors which are seldom found in his written work. As a class, correct these sentences in an informal situation.

One of the most effective procedures to follow in the oral correction of written errors is the informal teacher-student exchange:

TEACHER: (After placing sentence on board) Does this sentence contain an error? (To keep students on their toes, occasionally have students examine correct sentences. The answer to the above question should not always be yes.) "The teacher gave the students pencils and pen."

STUDENT: Yes. "Pen" is incorrect.

TEACHER: How can we correct this sentence?

STUDENT: Add an "s" to pen.

TEACHER: That is correct. We make pen plural by adding "s."

STUDENT: We could write the sentence in a different way. "The teacher gave the student a pencil and pen."

TEACHER: Yes, this sentence is also correct. All the nouns are now singular.

STUDENT: Singular?

TEACHER: Yes, singular. John, come to the desk, please, and select a *single* piece of paper from this stack. (You may develop the understanding of

the word further by talking about a single error
on Mary's paper, a single man, a singular idea,
etc.)

In this informal way, a teacher can develop an understanding of grammar in his class. However, some of the
students will need to be told over and over to correct the
same error. In such cases, brief self-made check lists to eliminate repeated errors are helpful. A class "never-again" list
of errors can also be a helpful aid to the young writer.

Probably the most effective method of all of the approaches for teaching grammar is the Writing-Grading-Cor-
rection-Discussion method. The student completes a writing
assignment, the teacher underlines the errors, the student
attempts to correct them, the teacher spends a few minutes
discussing the errors. He may decide on the individual approach if the error is not widespread, or he may choose the
group approach if the same error appears on more than one
paper. The written assignment may be any one of those
mentioned in the chapters on writing. They may be simple
sentences, compound or complex sentences, or paragraphs.
Regardless of the writing assignment, though, the teacher
must examine and grade the paper carefully if the writing
assignment is to have the full value intended. In fact, the
amount of benefit derived from writing assignments which
are given only a summary perusal is questionable.

GRAMMAR AND USAGE GAMES Grammar and usage
games are excellent teaching devices. Here are a few:

A. Give students a sample sentence, such as: "Because of the holiday, school was dismissed early."
Children are chosen—the first to represent the
first word slot, etc. Since "school" is a noun, the
first child will think of another noun substitu-
tion. The new sentence should have the same
pattern as the old one.

B. A variation of the above is to assign one student
the task of supplying all the noun substitutes,

another the verbs, etc. Students give the sentence as spontaneously as possible.

C. Try to express a thought or issue a command by using only nouns—only verbs—only prepositions, etc. Don't use sign language.

D. Choose a dialectical region in the U.S. and for an entire day, use the colloquialisms, dialect, and idioms peculiar to that area. (This assignment will require considerable work and planning, but it is a rewarding lesson.)

Usage

Usage can also be taught best when the need becomes obvious, as can mechanics and many other areas of language arts. Correct usage is an oral process, and is therefore best taught in an oral situation. It is most successful in the informal student-teacher exchange.

A study of dialects, colloquial expressions, regionalisms, and slang encourages better usage. Through such a study, students realize that if they are to reach the ultimate goals of oral communication—to understand and to be understood by as many people as possible—they must learn to speak correctly, eliminating major colloquialisms, slang, and little-known regionalisms from their speech. Some areas for study in this area are:

A. Find five examples of dialectical speech in *The Yearling* (M. K. Rawlings) or in other books which use dialectical speech. Discuss: Why are some of these examples of dialectical speech so difficult to understand?

B. Listen to your classmates speak. Make a list of colloquialisms they use.

Spelling

One of the best ways to give spelling relevance is to read two or three sentences to the class which contain new vocabulary words. Stress the importance of both spelling and handwriting. This dictation exercise should be repeated frequently.

Why Teach Poetry?

If your answer to the above question is "because it is in most curriculum textbooks," or "the principal suggests it," or "the students will have to know it later," don't bother to present poetry. If you have no interest in poetry and no intention of trying to develop an interest in it, don't try to teach it either. If, however, you enjoy poetry for what it is, an expressive art form which serves to stimulate interest in important ideas, often utilizing the emotions as a medium for involvement and offering appeal through novel settings and intriguing rhythm, *do teach it*. If you enjoy limericks, ballads, light or serious verse, Homeric or modern expression, try your hand at teaching it. Poetry, as well as the other areas of language arts, should be a part of the curriculum because of its immediate value. Future benefits will result naturally. The stress should be on enjoyment.

Let's get off to a good start. Compulsory memorization of poetry, poor selection, lack of enthusiasm, can spell failure and a permanent dislike for poetry. Choosing a concrete theme, appealing to the imagination, and steering clear of extreme sentimentality are some of the keys to a successful poetry program.

The poetry program must, of course, stress enjoyment. There is no better way to enjoy it than to listen to experts read selections. In some cases recordings made by the poet himself can be obtained. Students use these examples as models in their reading, listening, and interpretation. Poetry should be experimented with. Students, after developing an interest in poetry, can benefit from individual or group experimental reading of a wide selection of poetry. An attempt should be made by the teacher to develop an interest in all types of poetry—poetry ranging from the limericks of Ogden

Nash to the more serious works of such poets as Robert Frost and Carl Sandburg.

Experimenting with Poetry

There are many writing exercises which can accompany the study of poetry. But, an introductory one might be the description of the scene or mood set by a poem. "I Like to See It Lap the Miles" by Emily Dickinson is an excellent poem for this type of activity. Students should be given some experience writing their own poetry. This might involve just the reverse of the previous exercise. As a group, students set the mood and scene for the poem, then they proceed to write their poems or limericks. Light verse is probably the best motivation for this type of writing. Ogden Nash's poetry holds appeal for the young students and his rhyme pattern offers possibilities for student practice. In general, it is not necessary to stress meter and the technicalities of writing poetry in the elementary grades. It is often helpful to make the students aware of these elements, and then let students work with them if they like, but little more is necessary in this area until high school. If, indeed, our goal is to get children to appreciate poetry and other literature in the elementary school, work of a technical nature should be eliminated here, or at least minimized.

How Much Attention Shall We Give to the Poor or "Non"-Reader?

Students need to read a variety of materials, but "What can we do with the non-readers?" is a problem in virtually every language arts class.

One means of overcoming the non-reading problem is to first interest students in reading short newspaper and magazine articles, books with short, interesting excerpts, and even low vocabulary books written in comic-book style. Ask provocative questions which students can answer only by reading the selection suggested. To have success with activities of this nature, they should be kept on a voluntary basis. This exercise is most successful if it is adapted to a bulletin board.

NEWSPAPER AND MAGAZINE QUESTIONS AND STATEMENTS FOR USE:

a. According to _____, in_____, catching ducks in_____ is a year round sport.
b. Wolves are now found principally in_____.
c. Have you ever heard of a blue frog?
d. What's new on the seventh continent?

READING AND THE BULLETIN BOARD

Clip high-interest news articles from the newspaper and mount them attractively. Change them frequently to encourage continued reading. Encourage students to bring their own articles for display. Some classes appoint a student committee for this purpose.

BOOKS AND THE INDIVIDUAL

Each day, suggest one new book for reading. Students usually find paperbacks much more readable than hardbound editions. Very often, the cover sells the book.

WHY LEARN TO READ?

Before students will become good readers, they must have basic goals for learning to read and be sufficiently motivated to carry out at least some of them. Here are a few:
a. Information
b. Enjoyment
c. A broadened point of view
d. Future reading purposes

At least fifteen minutes should be allowed for individual reading in each language arts period. After all, one does learn to read by reading.

A BACKWARD GLANCE

Balance in the language arts program is paramount in importance. A balance of subject matter, of teacher techniques, and of new ideas (of which there can never be too many) must be reached.

It will be the new ideas that give life to the language arts program, and a teacher will do well to ask himself before each class, "What's new?" Whether it is a Langston Hughes poem, an opinionated letter to the editor from the local paper, or a writing assignment based on a provocative picture, *do something different!* A new bulletin board, an intriguing question on the chalk board, or a new book—these are all important elements in a creative classroom.

An experienced teacher remarked to her administrator while being reprimanded for her lack of creativity, "But, I've always taught this way."

"That," he replied, "is precisely the point I am making."

The teacher who spends a week teaching nothing but verbs, a week teaching compound sentences, a week teaching punctuation, etc. may teach some of the mechanics of language to his students, but he will certainly not teach students to think independently, to create, and to develop independence in all areas of study.

The successful language arts teacher exudes a deep appreciation for his subject material and for learning in general. The language arts teacher's scope is necessarily broader than that of a teacher in any other area of the curriculum, for a language arts teacher is concerned that his students be able to read a scientific magazine article with a reasonable degree of comprehension, to construct a study outline for his history class, and to understand the detailed language in a mathematical problem. But the language arts teacher's concern and responsibility go further than this. He must prepare the student for life situations. The student must know and be able to follow the rules for telephone conversations, for interviews, and if he is to be a useful citizen, he must be prepared to express his ideas clearly. He must be a critical listener and a critical reader. The language arts teacher is, in effect, a soothsayer. He must anticipate the oral and written language situations for which the student needs to be prepared, and if the student fails to gain skill in the language arts, he is sure to fail in his other learning attempts, thus reducing his potential as a successful citizen.

Index